Spirituality in Addictions Counseling:
A Clinician's Guide

H. Spencer O'Neal

MIDWATCH
PRESS

MidWatch Press
Apple Valley, California
Printed in the United States of America

ISBN-13: 978-0692952825
ISBN-10: 0692952829

Religion:
Is for people who don't want to go to hell

Spirituality:
Is for people who've been there

Dedicated to:

Caryn O'Neal

**with Love
and Gratitude**

Contents

- If a Spiritual Solution is the Answer, are Healthcare Professionals Necessary?
- Recovery - The Goal of Spiritually Based Counseling

- Source of Healing Power
- Counselor Qualifications
- Complex Problems - Simple Solutions
- Roadblocks to Successful Counseling
- Therapeutic Goal: Sustained Recovery

- Sources of Therapeutic Power
- General Counselor Attributes
- Attributes of a Biblical Counselor
- Attributes of and Techniques for Spiritually Based Addictions Counselors

- Is Sobriety Enough?
- Feelings of Disharmony in Sobriety
- Understanding and Internalizing 'God's' Love, and Signs of Recovery
- The Workings of the Spiritual Approach
- The Counselor's Therapeutic Ability is Based on Client Perception

- Research on the Effectiveness of Prayer
- Research Summary of Prayer

- Placebo and Nocebo Effects
- Background
- Placebo, Addiction, and Spirituality - Power Source Comparison
- Does Prayer Work?

- Three-fold Disease Concept
- Spiritual Awakening in 12 Step Programs
- Growing Medical Involvement in Recovery Treatment Programs

- Secular-Scientific Approach
- Religious-Biblical Approach
- Spiritual Approach
- A Counseling Technique for Finding "God"
- Placebo & Nocebo Effect, the Effectiveness of Prayer, and New Medical Considerations
- Spiritual Recovery
- Continuing Support

Preface

How to most effectively deal with alcoholism and other addictions has been a dilemma nearly as old as humankind itself. Until the advent of Alcoholics Anonymous (A.A.) in 1935 no consistently effective remedy had been discovered. Alcoholics Anonymous presented a non-scientific, non-religious, spiritually based approach to the treatment of alcoholism that has a self-proclaimed success rate of over fifty percent. This experiential statistic became evident with the publication of the Second Edition of the book Alcoholics Anonymous in 1955. A.A. does not maintain statistics of individual membership. As such, empirically accurate statistical studies are not possible. However, what was available in 1955 was the experience of its estimated 150,000 members, its rate of growth, and its proliferation to 6,000 groups since A.A.'s inception 20 years earlier. These statistics are noted in the forward to the Second Edition of the book "Alcoholics Anonymous" as such:

"…. Public acceptance of A.A. grew by leaps and bounds. For this there were two principal reasons: the large numbers of recoveries, and reunited homes. These made their impressions everywhere. Of alcoholics who came to A.A. and really tried, 50% got sober at once and remained that way; 25% sobered up after some relapses, and among the remainder, those who stayed on with A.A. showed improvement. Other thousands came to a few A.A. meetings and at first decided they didn't want the program. But great numbers of these -about two out of three- began to return as time passed." (Anonymous, 2001, pp.xv-xxiii)

1

In 2001 there were over 2 million members, 100,800 groups, in 150 countries. Although there is much speculation concerning the actual success rate of A.A., today the experiential statistics noted in 1955 appear to be remain true, that of those who *come* to A.A. *and really try*, well over fifty percent will recover. [Of those *sent* to A.A. and *refuse to try*, statistics are less positive, but some do recover.] The approach used that garnered such success in the recovery program outlined in the book "Alcoholics Anonymous" was a *spiritual* one. This approach is not to be construed as a religious approach, and certainly differs from a secular approach. Both religious and secular approaches had been tried for many millennia with little to no success. What differs in the spiritual approach? And why does it appear to be effective in treating those with addictions?

This book seeks to answer those and other questions by a review of current literature. It will attempt to examine the secular, religious, and spiritual approaches to counseling and determine the *goal, power, and methodologies* of each approach in relation to achieving the initial and primary aim of addictions counseling, which, unlike other types of therapeutic interventions, involves the total abstinence from addictive substances and/or the complete cessation of addictive behaviors.

This review determined that the spiritual approach to addictions recovery was the most effective therapeutic approach of those researched. Some counseling techniques that may be helpful to the clinician were included. Ancillary studies were also incorporated in order to review their possible relevance with regard to the concept of therapeutic spiritual healing and spiritual living. Those studies involved the influence of placebos and nocebos, and the effects of intercessory and personal prayer. These studies were included in order to examine the effects these influences may have on the client, in that some clinicians might infer that the spiritual approach may be the result of, or strongly influenced by, these other factors.

Finally, recent findings implying that addictions alter brain structure, has led medical science to now consider alcoholism, and other addictions, a *medical/physical* diagnosis and thus no longer consider them as conditions to be treated primarily through psychiatric means. Such a shift in this diagnostic process will give rise to variations in treatment options and philosophies. It will alter the medical profession's perception of addictions from a mental health disease/disorder to a predominantly medically treatable disease concept. Implications of this philosophical shift are explored.

It should be noted here that, with the entrance of medical science into the field of addictions treatment, along with its alteration of diagnostic considerations from psychiatric to medical, the qualification criteria for clinicians who engage in the treatment of individuals with addictions is beginning to change as well. Since its inception, Alcoholics Anonymous has promulgated its experience regarding the attributes of those who are generally successful in treating alcoholics. Similar experiences also tend to apply to those with related addictions. A.A.'s experience indicates that alcoholics will rarely discuss their situation honesty with doctors, psychiatrists, therapists, counselors, clergy, etc. However, another alcoholic, who has recovered, who offers a solution, can usually intercede successfully with an alcoholic within a very brief period of time. (Anonymous, 2001, p. 18). As such, since its founding until present, with few exceptions, addictions counselors have been selected from the ranks of those who have found personal recovery from their own addiction(s). Most of these counselors have been trained and certified as addictions counselors and have years of successful experience, but few have obtained additional formal education as licensed clinical mental health professionals. Yet, these addictions counselors have performed their therapeutic roles exceptionally well and guided their clients to improved lives and lasting recoveries.

With greater frequency state governments are beginning to look toward requiring addictions counselors to obtain more formal education, hold a degree in a mental health related field, and receive specialty training in, or be certified as, an Addictions Therapist. With these new requirements, more traditionally and formally educated counselors are beginning to enter the addictions field. Few of these new counselors have experienced addictions themselves or recovered from alcoholism or a related addictive disorder. *Hence, the medical and psychiatric communities will again be faced with the age-old problem of gaining the trust and confidence of, and effectively communicating with, their clients with addictions.* This book should be of assistance to those secular and/or religion based counselors who are entering the field of addictions counseling.

Although this book is addressed specifically to addictions counselors, it should be noted that the spiritual approach outlined here can be useful in other areas of therapeutic counseling as well. The spiritual approach is designed to facilitate an overall change in lifestyle for the client. A change in lifestyle is necessary because - *addictions are forever*. Therefore, by necessity, the *solution* for the addiction must be forever as well. So far, the only effective long term solution to the age-old riddle of alcoholism, and other addictive disorders, is one that is *internalized* and *spiritual*.

It should be noted here that a subtle but significant difference exists between alcoholism and other addictive disorders. Though treatment of these addictions may be similar, this book separately annotates alcoholism from other addictions. (O'Neal, H., 2011).

Chapter 1

The Purpose of this Book: Explore the Spiritual Approach to Addictions Counseling

Why Spirituality? (For people who have been to hell)

The purpose of this book is to explore the *Spiritual Approach to Addictions Therapy*. With the advent and near universal acceptance of the 'scientific method' for the study of all proposed hypothetical methods of medical and mental health treatments, the spiritual approach had diminished to the point of near non-existence. The mention of treatments containing a *spiritual* element, or elements originating from "the realm of grace and faith," were considered scientific heresy and often viewed as ignorant superstition. (Jones, 2006). This evolution of thought is to some degree understandable in man's efforts to come to grips with his own 'being' and 'workings' on a purely intellectual plane - without resorting to an intangible 'God' as the answer to all things heretofore unexplainable.

However, on June 10, 1935, the day Doctor Bob Smith, an Akron, Ohio physician, took his last drink of alcohol, and though no one realized it at the time, the founding of Alcoholics Anonymous had occurred. With this one seemingly insignificant event, a *Spiritual Approach* to the age-old scourge of alcoholism had commenced its re-entry into the field of therapeutic mental health

5

practice. As quoted in "The Medical View on A.A.," Dr. Foster Kennedy, neurologist, capitulated to this conclusion by indicating that if the scientific (medical) profession is not cognizant and appreciative of "religion" (spirituality) and "association" "…We shall stand convicted of emotional sterility and of having lost the faith that moves mountains, without which medicine can do little." (Anonymous, 2001, pp. 569-570)

In this book, the concept of 'God' is often used interchangeably with the term 'Spirituality.' Although the phraseology of 'religion' may at times appear, the term is used typically to denote an institution that has a 'Higher Power' at its center and not to assume a specific dogmatic practice, unless otherwise indicated. An adage often heard in spiritually based recovery programs is: "Religion is for people who don't want to go to hell; Spirituality is for people who have been there."

Religion connotes then the study of a particular deity centered dogmatic belief system through the use of histories, scriptures, and traditions. *Spirituality* implies the acceptance and internalization of an unseen *Power*, of mysterious origin, that has rescued a fallen soul from the depths of a seemingly inescapable abyss. *Religion* then denotes the gaining of knowledge of a particular system of belief in a deity, as taught by others. Whereas *spirituality* indicates an actual abiding 'faith' in a *Power* Greater than one's self and that that 'faith' is based on the experience of actually being 'saved' by that *Spiritual* Entity - often without any prior knowledge of who or what that *Power* might be. It should be noted here that it is generally the goal of various 'religions' to bring their adherents to the point of spiritual awakening through their teachings of 'God.' Conversely, it is often the case that those who have had a vital *Spiritual* encounter seek to then know their 'Rescuer' better by religious study and participation.

Discussion of the Three Basic Approaches to Therapy

This book will explore the three most common approaches to Addictions Therapy. It will also examine the basic goal; role of the counselor; source of therapeutic power; and outcome expectations of each therapeutic approach. Since the founding of Alcoholics Anonymous, its spiritually based therapeutic interventions seem to have been successful in addictions counseling whereas other interventions appear to have consistently failed. This book will attempt to shed light on why the spiritual approach seems to produce results, where the medical, secular-scientific and religious approaches have made only minimal headway.

By its nature, this book's examination of a spiritual approach to counseling, will conjure up bias and preconceived ideas in many researchers. Nevertheless, this book proposes to observe and report on therapeutic practices that produce significantly positive results. The authors of the book "Alcoholics Anonymous" also discussed such predetermined concepts in its chapter titled "We Agnostics" where it describes that the purpose of their book is to help the reader discover a "Power Greater than ourselves" and that, as such, it will be "spiritual and moral." "And it means, of course, that we are going to talk about God." (Anonymous, 2001, p. 45). For the edification of interested clinicians, an examination of the *Spiritual Approach*, in relation to the other approaches mentioned, is the purpose of this book.

Three Approaches Defined

For purposes of background footing, this book will examine three basic approaches to general therapeutic psychological counseling. These three approaches are Secular-Scientific, Biblical-

Religious, and Spiritual. Although religions other than those of Judeo-Christian heritage may offer counseling assistance for their adherents, the use of alcohol and other intoxicants is typically forbidden in their writings. (Breining, et al., 2008, p. 30). Therefore they will not be specifically addressed here. Also not definitely addressed in this book are Native American Spiritual practices. Although very therapeutic, the techniques used are beyond the scope of this current work. As such, religious based counseling practices discussed in this research will be from a Christian - Biblical perspective.

Defining the Problem and the Goal of the Solution

An issue that each of the three approaches has grappled with, and one that persists to this day, is that of first *defining the problem,* and then *defining the goal* of therapy. Although it is not the premise of this book to explore these issues in-depth, for the sake of clarification to the addictions counselor, they should be explained briefly now: Clients will present to the clinical setting with a variety of complaints that appear unrelated an underlying addiction. In such cases, their addiction may have initially started as a mechanism used to cope with their problems, or their presenting problems may be the result of their addiction. In either event, once the *problem* has been defined, and it is determined that a chemical addiction is present, then that dependency issue must be substantially addressed prior to tackling any other presenting problems. As such, if the client has met the criteria for dependence, then total abstinence will be the *goal* of therapy as: "the research shows clearly that 'moderation' is unlikely to be successful for patients who already meet criteria for dependence, whether defined by the DSM-IV (American Psychiatric Association, 2000) or by a variety of assessment tools" (Harvard Medical School, 1-2009). Therefore, the interest and scope of this book is restricted to *abstinence* from addictive substances as being *the* therapeutic *goal* sought of addictions counseling, regardless of the therapeutic approach utilized.

What is Counseling's Source of Therapeutic Power?

Psychology is defined as: "The scientific study of the mind, its activities, and human and animal behavior." Counseling is defined as: "Professional guidance of the individual by utilizing psychological methods especially in collecting case history data, using various techniques of the personal interview, and testing interests and aptitudes." (Merriam-Webster, 1999). These definitions are incorporated into all three of the approaches to counseling being examined. However, the addictions therapist should have a basic idea of how each approach differs in their views of psychology and therapeutic-clinical counseling. Nevertheless, the central focus of this book is on the spiritual approach and an examination of its unprecedented successes in assisting alcoholics, and those with other addictions, to recover, whereas the effectiveness of other methods have proven to be nominal at best.

Although the basic counseling methodology for all three approaches is similar, the eventual outcome and source of therapeutic power differs significantly. A recent study on this topic stated: "Today's mental health system is largely a product of western science. Like a one-eyed giant, it has great power, but it lacks the wisdom which makes life sacred and meaningful." (Blanch, 2007). In other words, the mental health system has made great strides in delving into the human psyche and attempting to make adjustments. This is all well and good, but it is also sterile and strictly clinical. It lacks the *sacred power* which makes *meaning* of life, and makes life meaningful.

The primary therapeutic source of *power* for the effective addictions clinician should be *spiritual* in nature. The Christian counselor obviously relies on a religious source of therapeutic *power*. The secular-scientific counselor understandably relies solely on scientific methods. However, it is the counselors themselves who are often perceived by the client as possessing *the* source of healing power. For the biblical and spiritual approaches, this perception will need to be addressed by both counselor and client during the therapeutic process.

With Sobriety,
All Else
Is Possible

Chapter 2

The Secular-Scientific Counseling Approach

The definition of the *Scientific Method*: "Principles and procedures for the systematic pursuit of knowledge involving the recognition and formulation of a problem, the collection of data through observation and experiment, and the formulation and testing of hypotheses." (Merriam-Webster, 1999).

The Power Source for Secular-Scientific Counseling

The secular-scientific approach to counseling utilizes various 'schools' of thought and practice, techniques and ideologies derived from individual researchers and practitioners who have produced theories and methods which they believe, if used in their counseling practices, will be therapeutic to their clients. The sole source of *power* within the secular-scientific model of counseling is that projected from the client themselves. An old joke in the field of psychology pertains here: "How many psychotherapists does it take to change a light bulb?" Answer: "Only one, but the bulb must want to be changed." Of course, the therapist can project the illusion of power into the relationship and attempt to control the perception of the client, but clients must *perceive* that the therapist has the *power* to help them with their difficulties. As such, the ultimate *power* in the secular therapeutic relationship lies within the client's *perception* and/or *projection* of healing power into the therapist.

The Goal of Secular-Scientific Counseling

The characteristic *goal* of secular therapy is to assist the client in alleviation of particular symptoms or emotional distress which induces physical or mental discomfort or difficulty. In most cases, the counseling goal is to bring the client into harmony with self. In this process of self-awareness, often called "affirmation" therapy, the client is led to view self as justified in feelings and behaviors despite being out of sync with societal norms. It is for this reason that the secular-scientific approach to therapy often fails with addictive disorders in that affirming the client in their addiction, or in continuation in thoughts and behaviors that may be unrelated, but have helped perpetuate the emotions behind their addiction(s), is counterproductive. This type of secular therapy has a tendency to instill an introspective "value system" in the client which then is likely to breed "self-absorption, narcissism, and the tendency to interpret everything in individual terms." (Goode & Wagner, 1993, pp. 7-8). It may also breed codependency in the clinician.

Although independent thought has always held sway in the reasoning's of men, during the late 19th and early 20th centuries, scientific thought, method, and practice began replacing God's laws as the benchmark of foundational knowledge. By the 1930's secular psychotherapeutic practices and approaches were reportedly making significant strides in the classification, diagnosis, and treatment of many mental health problems, yet they could make no appreciable progress with the field of addictions recovery. (Goode & Wagner, 1993, pp. 3-4) However, it should be noted that at that time, "when researchers first began to investigate what caused addictive behavior, they believed that people with developed addictions were somehow morally flawed or lacking in willpower." It was believed that "punishment" or "willpower" were the tools necessary to help the client "break the habit." (Harvard Medical School, 7-2011).

Dr. Carl Jung is quoted in the book "Alcoholics Anonymous" as stating to an alcoholic client: "You have the mind of a chronic alcoholic. I have never seen one single case recover, where that state of mind existed to the extent that it does in you." During that time period, the early 1930's, the recoveries secular practitioners witnessed, were those in which patients reported having had a "vital spiritual experience." (Anonymous, 2001, p. 27). Dr. Jung related to his client that he had been attempting to steer him into having a spiritual experience, but that such guidance was outside of his realm of expertise. The spiritually based recoveries noted by Dr. Jung, or recoveries attributed to the intervention of a "Higher Power," were baffling to the scientific community in that these spiritual recoveries violated the methodology of measurable and observable, cause and effect, relationships that secular scholars adhered to as the sole test of *truth*. These scientists observed and reported seemingly miraculous spiritually based recoveries, but could not quantify why or how the spiritual approach worked after their "measured" scientific approaches failed. Nor did their scientific training prepare them to facilitate such spiritually based transformations and recoveries. Science has essentially turned a blind eye to the successes achieved through use of the spiritual approach and often ostracizes those who would attempt to explain it and/or capitalize on its successes even for the well-being and recovery of their clients.

Perspectives on Truth

Remarkably, the goal of arriving at *truth* is the very essence of both religious and secular scientists. Religious scientific investigators look for 'truth' by attempting to locate and affirm

13

God's order, design, and plan, in their research. Conversely, secular scientists specifically disavow any conclusions that point toward the existence of a Creative Intelligence and believe that 'truth' can only be 'true' if its results and observations are intellectually hypothesized and consistently predictable. The fallacy of this concept is that the secular-scientific method inevitably leads to the conclusion that the ability of man to *reason* is in itself the central focal point of the universe. As such, man would be god. If this were the case, and man's reasoning superior, then the question arises why man's scientific reasoning has been unable to cure alcoholism and why it is unable to explain why the spiritual approach has achieved a significant degree of success? What is the *origin* of *reason*?

Effectiveness of Secular-Scientific Approaches

In discussing the effectiveness of psychotherapy Robert Bellah; et al., in their 1985 volume "Habits of the Heart," indicate that the acceptance of the psychotherapeutic ethic has produced a decline in traditional (Spiritually based) values postulating that the secular psycho-ethic value system has produced "an individual who is able to be the source of his own standards" and "denies all forms of obligation and commitment in relationships." (Goode & Wagner, 1993, p. 8). This egocentric approach may show promise in some types of therapy, however, in stark contrast to Bellah's philosophy is a saying which is typically directed toward newer, more ego-centered members entering 12 Step recovery programs. That saying is: "There is a God, and it's not you." The *truth* is that for those with addictions, there *is* a power greater than themselves. That *power* is their addiction. Although initially clients may not fully comprehend the nature of their difficulty, they seek therapy in an attempt to overcome the *power* of their addictions. Despite the secular-scientific philosophy that individuals can overcome their difficulties through the tapping of their own inner willpower, the power actually being tapped is that of the therapist, or the client's projection of power into the therapist. This power may be effective in treating some client difficulties; however, the *power* of the therapist has been proven to hold little permanent sway over the *power* of addictions.

It's been over a century since the widespread acceptance of the scientific method in the early 20th century. Still the secular/clinical mental health field is trying to prove itself and its methods as valid, reliable, meaningful, and worthwhile. Psychoanalysis was thought to be the approach of choice through the 1940's and 50's; Behaviorism was prominent in the 60's; Humanist theories were supreme in the 70's; Psychodynamic and Cognitive Approaches gained strength in the 80's and 90's; and a combination of Cognitive and Behavioral Therapies (CBT), Motivational Interviewing (MI), and Mindfulness, are currently accepted as the therapeutic models of choice. However, despite numerous studies as to their effectiveness, no particular theory or therapeutic method has demonstrated successful results superior to any other secular theory or practice. The implication of this, is that all secular approaches are mildly to moderately effective to a certain degree. However, no secular therapeutic approach has been definitively shown to provide success beyond that point. As such, most clinicians are "eclectic" meaning they tend to pick and choose and integrate schools of practice to fit their needs, as one approach typically works just as well as the other. (Goode & Wagner, 1993, pp. 3-4).

Certainly great strides have been made in the therapeutic process, secular and otherwise, but although some successes outside of the addictions field are demonstrable, there is no consensus on which of the numerous accepted theories: Rogerian, Freudian, Jungian, Behavioral, CBT, MI, etc., etc., are most successful, or why. More recent reports indicate that "finding a reliable treatment for alcoholism has been a frustrating quest. In the best studies, all common psychosocial approaches have been found equally and only moderately effective" (Harvard Medical School, 7-2005). In other words, trials of all secular-scientific methods have produced results that are moderately better than doing nothing at all. Additionally, none of these methods has proven to be superior to any other, and none have shown themselves to produce results approaching those achieved through spiritual means.

With Sobriety,
All Else
Is Possible

Chapter 3

The Religious Counseling Approach

The definition of *Dogma*: "Something held as an established opinion; especially a definite authoritative tenet; a code of such tenets (pedagogical dogma); a point of view or tenet put forth as authoritative without adequate (scientific) grounds; a doctrine or body of doctrines concerning faith or morals formally stated and authoritatively proclaimed by a church; a belief or set of beliefs that is taught by a religious organization." (Merriam-Webster, 1999).

The Power Source for the Religious Counseling Approach

Although some initial basic counseling techniques are typically used as standard therapeutic practice, the *power* and *goals* of the *religious approach* differ greatly from the secular-scientific. The religious approach to counseling may utilize various 'denominational' dogmatic beliefs, practices, and ideologies as its value system or benchmark from which individual thoughts, practices, and behaviors can be compared. For example, in a Christian counseling setting, the predominant source of *power* is Christ or God. Both the therapist and the client have a mutual belief and faith in the God of the Bible as viewed from their own particular denominational (or non-denominational) perspective. The therapist is typically viewed by clients, not as a source of healing power, but as a guide to assist them in more closely understanding God's expectations of them and to direct them in the process of more closely adhering to the religious view of God's will. A caution for Christian counselors however, is that clients often view them as possessing exceptional knowledge of their religious faith and hold them up as examples of virtuous perfection for clients to emulate.

The Goal of the Religious Counseling Approach

The *goal* of religious based therapy is to facilitate the client's recognition of their wrongs, and confession of their 'sins.' The further goal is then to help the client comprehend and appreciate God's unconditional love, God's *power* and willingness to forgive sins, and God's desire that the client attempt to live his or her life without repeating the same or similar offenses. This feeling of being reconciled, of being at peace with God, has been shown to possess exceptional restorative *power.* The therapeutic *power* of the religious approach resides with *God.* This approach has proven to be effective in addictions counseling for those clients who adhere to a specific religious denominational faith and follow its precepts; and/or have faith in and follow a denominational pastor whom they believe will guide them faithfully to the source of God's restorative power.

Bill Wilson, a co-founder of Alcoholics Anonymous gained his initial sobriety through this religious based therapeutic method as delineated for him by Ebby Thacher using the principles of the Oxford Group. Bill related his experience as:

"...I humbly offered myself to God, as I then I understood Him, to do with me as He would. I placed myself unreservedly under His care and direction. I admitted for the first time that of myself I was nothing; that without Him I was lost. I ruthlessly faced my *sins* and became *willing* to have my new-found Friend take them

away, root and branch. I have not had a drink since."
(*emphasis* added) (Anonymous, 2001, p. 13).

The religion based type of therapy seeks to instill an intrinsic "value system" which then tends to provide the client with external guidelines to follow. In-so-doing the client will be inclined to loosen his or her grip on ego, attempt to be more tolerant of others, and become more open to altering behavioral patterns that may be physically and/or emotionally harmful to themselves or others. As the client acts more positively toward the world, the world appears to react more positively in-kind to the client.

Effectiveness of the Religious Approach

As we can see, the religious approach to addictions counseling may prove to be very effective. However, the obvious drawback to this approach is that it typically works best for those clients who are adherents of, or are feeling drawn to a specific denominational faith or belief that is the same as, or similar to that of the counselor. The denominational faith or religious viewpoint of the therapist does not have to align with the client, but great care must be taken with regard to dogmatic sensitivities should the therapist's and client's theological beliefs differ.

Some current religious oriented, or faith based, recovery programs offer treatment to those who suffer from addictions but include, and often require, denominational religious training as part of their recovery program. As such, the counselor, often a pastor, is educating the client in that pastor's own particular niche of religious dogma while simultaneously providing therapy for the client's addictions. In fairness though, such programs often do not require a specific denominational religious commitment, but rather only offer a basic educational study in Christian religious biblical principles. These programs attempt to lead the client to a greater understanding of the healing power of the God of the Bible. Again, this approach is often effective, but it is not conducive for inclusion in general training programs for addictions counselors. Nevertheless, addictions counselors may do well to guide clients to include their own particular religious denominational faith into their personal recovery programs as a source of healing power. Ongoing spiritual growth is a necessity of quality long-term recovery.

With Sobriety,
All Else
Is Possible

Chapter 4

An Exploration of Spirituality

Reason vs. Spirit

"Science without religion is lame, religion without science is blind."
— Albert Einstein

Is 'truth' God's, or man's? Is the search for truth an actual search for *truth* wherever that truth may be, or is it an agenda driven search for grandiosity and egoism by the researcher? In reality, it appears that God's 'truth' is constant and unchanging, whereas secular-scientific 'truth' is in a constant state of flux, as one discovery often negates what was previously regarded as 'truth.' (Jones, 2006). An example of this evolution of 'truth' is pointed out in the chapter titled "We Agnostics" (Anonymous, 2001, p. 51) which states:

"Even in the present century, American newspapers were afraid to print an account of the Wright Brothers' first successful flight at Kitty Hawk. Had not all efforts at flight failed before? Did not Professor Langley's flying machine go to the bottom of the Potomac River? Was it not true that the best mathematical minds had proved man could never fly?"

Even in the face of such glowing failures of the scientific method, in his book regarding Biblical Christian counseling, "The

21

Counsel of Heaven on Earth: Foundations for Biblical Christian Counseling," Dr. Ian Jones states: "Modern scientific inquiry has developed meticulous methods that generally rest on a belief in a universe of natural cause and effect that views the realm of grace and faith as supercilious fantasy… Hence… faith, theology, and religion should either recognize *scientific knowledge as the supreme arbiter of reality* or stay on their own nonscientific turf of rituals and church dogma while maintaining a policy of noninterference." (emphasis added) (Jones, 2006, p. 5).

Similarly, in a June 30, 2011 statement on theology by Pope Benedict XVI, then leader of the Roman Catholic Church (Benedict XVI, 2011), discussed two types of reason. One type that is incompatible with faith, and one that is open to the pondering of life itself. The Christian leader indicated that the first type of scientific reasoning discards everything that falls outside of that which can be scientifically verified. This type of reason wants to subject God to experimentation. This first type of scientific reasoning the Holy Father termed, "violentia rationis," or "the despotism of reason," and stated that it (reason) attempts to be *"The supreme and ultimate judge of everything"* (emphasis added).

The second type of scientific reasoning joins with faith and includes man's continuing search for ultimate truth and love. Neither of these most human elements is able to be reliably proven or disproven through the scientific method. Hence, the Pontiff noted this second type of reasoning is necessary for contemplation of "The great questions regarding man himself." The Pope said: "Love wants to know better the one it loves. Love, true love, does not make one blind but seeing. Part of it is a thirst for knowledge, true knowledge of the other."

The Pontiff related that the first approach to scientific reasoning has led to great accomplishments, "And no one would dare to seriously deny that this approach is right and necessary in the realm of knowledge of nature and of its laws." "However," he said, "such a use of reason has a limit: God is not an object of human experimentation. He is Subject and manifests himself only in the *person to person* relationship, which is part of the *essence of person*" (emphasis added). In other words, since *reason* has not created life, it has no measurable components for involvement in spiritual human to human relationships. Only the *Creative Spirit* of God can have meaningful encounters with the *Animating Spirit* within humankind. *Reason* learns of itself by dissecting the dead, whereas *Spirit* is *life* and *It* knows that *It is*. Life is capable of understanding reason, but reason is incapable of understanding the essence of life.

Who am I? Why am I here?

Therefore, for purposes of this book, it may be assumed that *Spirituality* is construed as: the *Spirit* of Humankind; And, the *Spirit* of a "Power Greater than Ourselves" (God); Seeking each other through a strong mutual desire to honestly *know* (truth), *join* (relationship), and *love* (fulfillment), each-other. This innate desire to know one's spiritual self is often voiced in man's age-old questions when seeking to know one's place in the Universe: "Who am I?" and "Why am I here?" These questions appear to be answered in simple terms in the book "Alcoholics Anonymous:"

"If what we have learned and felt and seen means anything at all, it means that all of us, whatever our race, creed, or color are the *children of a living Creator* with whom we may form a relationship upon simple and understandable terms as soon as we are willing and honest enough to try."

Being a "Child of God" certainly appears as a simplistic answer to such in-depth conceptual questions regarding the nature of human existence. Nonetheless, it is *the* answer. But how then does one put this answer into meaningful practice? The book further explains:

"This is the how and the why of it. First of all, we had to quit playing God. It didn't work. Next, we decided that hereafter in this drama of life, God was going to be our Director. He is the Principal; we are His agents. He is the Father, and we are His children. Most good ideas are simple, and this concept was the keystone of the new and triumphant arch through which we passed to freedom." (Anonymous, 2001, pp. 28, 62).

From a counselor's perspective then: if 'God' (Spirituality) is to be a directing force in the lives of clients, further emphasis then would be necessary to determine the nature of *spiritual principles* as a framework within which further action should be contemplated.

God is Truth – Truth is God

Truth. Truth is the foundation of wellness. Truth is the destination striven to be achieved in all therapeutic counseling. Truth is the central focus of all that is sought. From the perspective of *faith* and *spirituality*, God, or the realm of the Creative Spirit, *is Truth.* Conversely, 'Truth' is *God.* Thus, all truth belongs to the Creator. In around 388 A.D., St. Augustine wrote that "Every good is from God. There is no nature, therefore, which is not from God. That movement, however, of turning away from God is what we acknowledged as sin, because it is a defective movement and every defect is from nothing. See whence it comes, and you may be certain that it does not come from God." As human beings then we often tend to feel that if God is truth, and He sees all and knows all, why

24

then does evil occur? Or why, if He loves us, why doesn't He just 'heal' us or at least prevent us from doing wrong - or prevent wrong from happening? St Augustine further states that "Just as you do not, by your memory of them, compel past events to have happened, neither does God, by His foreknowledge, compel future events to take place. And just as you remember certain things which you have done, but have not done all that you remember, so too God foreknows all the things of which He is the Author, but He is not Himself the Author of all that He foreknows." (St. Augustine, 1979).

This truth that is from God then, is that He set all things in motion. Yet, He did not predetermine the outcome of all things. Although, He delineated precise natural law for the physical universe and instinctual actions and reactions for lower life forms, for human beings, He gave *free-will*. His desire in so doing is for the opportunity of mutual, shared love; God's love being universal; humankind's love, conditional. In other words, God desires us, in truth and love, to choose Him and willingly remain with Him. With reference to Moses' proclamation of God's word to his people "I have set before you, life and death, the blessing and the curse. Choose life then that you … may live by loving the Lord,… heeding His voice, and holding fast to Him" (NAB, 2002)(Deut 30:19-20).

St. Justin Martyr stated that:

> "Chastisments and good rewards are distributed according to the merit of each man's actions. Were this not the case, and were all things to happen according to the decree of fate, there would be nothing at all in our power. If fate decrees that this man is to be good, and that one wicked then neither is the former to be praised nor the latter to be blamed… If the human race does not have the power of a freely deliberated choice in fleeing evil and

25

in choosing good, then men are not accountable for their actions, whatever they may be. ... God did not make man like the other beings, the trees and the four-legged beasts, for example, which cannot do anything by free choice. Neither would man deserve reward or praise if he did not of himself choose the good; nor, if he acted wickedly, would he deserve punishmenet, since he would not be evil by choice, and could not be other than that which he was born." "Choose the good." (St. Justin, 1970)

Is Punishment from God?

The Old Testament legalistic language tone of Moses tends to 'feel' harsh when one is looking to the spiritual nature of 'God' in a current day Addictions Counseling setting. However, when the truth and love of the underlying concept is examined, one can see that "God," the "Power Greater than ourselves," has granted mankind, *free-will*. 'Free-will' is the power to *choose* one's own destiny, the ability to make mistakes, the abiltiy to find one's own way, the ability to act on impulse, greed, reason, sacrifice, love, hate, lust, or any number of emotions, thoughts, or motives. Addictions hijack personal choice and free-will. However, God has planted within the human psyche, a *Spirit*, and a basic understanding of right and wrong. The book "Alcoholics Anonymous" states: "...for deep down in every man, woman, and child, is the fundamental idea of God. It may be obscured by calamity, by pomp, by worship of other things, but in some form or other it is there." (Anonymous, 2001, p. 55).*

[*Note: The reader may ask: Is the book Alcoholics Anonymous an inspired text from where God speaks to humankind? 'No.' Although some claim they believe the book to be "inspired" based on it's worldwide results, the book Alcoholics Anonymous is merely a set of experiential observations of what has occurred over time. It describes, and attempts to explain, in layman's terms how the *Spirit* of *Good* has overcome the Spirit of alcohol(ism). It also describes from the viewpoint of experience, how some people with hopeless conditions, who have tried every conceivable alternative treatment, without success, have discovered a Power greater that themselves – and more importantly – a Power greater than their addiction, which solved their problem. The book describes how this Power was discovered and tapped by the early members of A.A., who subsequently recovered. The book is an explanation of how this was accomplished. As such, if the reader desires *'a'* method of recovery from their addiction, the book suggests a proven method for doing so. There is nothing obligitory about it. However, counselors of clients with addictions, are not serving their clients well if they choose to ignore this proven program of recovery and the practical spiritual precepts outlined in the book, Alcoholic Anonymous.]

This *internal* fundamental idea of "God" intuitively knows the right choice from the wrong. "...Our problems were of our own making. Bottles were only a symbol." (Anonymous, 2001, p. 103). When *wrong* choices, borne of *self*, are continually in conflict with what is intuitively known as *right*, internal strife and unsettledness becomes apparent. This *unsettledness* of self is believed to be the "punishment" so often refered to in religious teachings. If viewed from this perspective, God did not punish Judas for his betrayal of Christ. Judas' internal *unsettledness*, which resulted from his actions, caused him to inflict his own punishment. Judas could no longer live with the self-recriminations over his own actions. Along similar lines, in contemplation of avoiding this unsettledness, the book "Alcoholics Anonymous" described its view of God's desire for mankind as:

"We are sure God wants us to be happy, joyous, and free. We cannot subscribe to the belief that this life is a vale of tears, though it once was just that for many of us. But it is clear that we made our own misery. God didn't do it. Avoid then, the deliberate manufacture of misery, but if trouble comes, cheerfully capitalize it as an opportunity to demonstrate His omnipotence." (Anonymous, 2001, p. 133).

This fundamental concept sheds a whole new light on the thinking of those with addictive disorders. Life doesn't just happen to people. People have the option of making choices that can alter the emotional outcome of any situation they might encounter. It's not what happens to people, it's how they react to what happens to them, that determines how they feel inside. Reflecting on what 'God's' 'Spirit within' would have people *do,* assists them to make *right* choices and, in so doing, they are then avoiding the manufacture of their own misery. They then describe finding themselves on the road to being happy and emotionally content.

These *right* choices are often not the easiest choices to make in the moment. But people usually find that, over the course of time, right choices prove to be the easiest, the most satisfactory, and the most rewarding after all. They begin to understand these are the choices that 'God' would want them to make. As such, right choices are *always* in their own best interest. Their appropriate choices tend to bring people into closer contact with their Creator. They find that all 'God' desires of them is that they *choose* to be closer to Him. *Free-will* then, may be viewed as something 'God' bestowed upon humankind, not so that people would dutifully worship Him, but that they might choose to commune with Him and follow His ways and principles. 'God' provides *His children* with free-will in hopes that they will *choose* Him. He does not predestine their choice.

28

Chapter 5

The Spiritual Counseling Approach

In review: 1) The goal of the *secular-scientific approach* to counseling is to assist the client in abstaining from their addictive behaviors and to affirm '*self*.' The client's addiction is not viewed as sinful, but rather a behavior that is either excessive, illegal, or both. The source of therapeutic *power* in the secular-scientific approach is that which is projected into the counselor by the client. 2) The goal of the *religious approach* to addictions counseling is to assist the client in recognizing their sinfulness, obtaining forgiveness, and finding the 'God' of their particular denominational faith/religion. Drunkenness and addictions are sinful in the eyes of many religions. Thus, addictions are viewed as sin and not as a disease. As such, abstinence is a secondary goal to turning away from sin. The source of healing power in the religious approach is 'God,' as understood by the particular religious denomination of the counselor and client.

The Power Source for the Spiritual Counseling Approach

Of necessity, the *spiritual approach* of counseling utilizes techniques and ideologies from both the scientific and the religious realms. However, the aim of the spiritual counseling approach is to bring the client's internal *animating spirit* of '*self*' into *attunement* with the *Spirit* of the Universe, or the 'God' personal to the nature of the client. The animating spirit is that force or essence which brings *life* into the body. The body can be complete, whole, and in good working order, but without the animating, life giving spirit or *soul*, the body is *dead*. In blunt terms, one can attempt to *reason* with a *life-less* body all one wishes, but without the yet undefinable, miraculous, life giving Spiritual force, about which this book is discussing, the body will remain unresponsive or 'dead.' Though it is true that neither the counselor, the client, nor anyone else, can create or generate this *life* giving force, it is also true that the client can be assisted to come into closer contact with *It*. In other words, the client can be assisted to come into conscious contact with this Animating Spirit, - or: 'God.' For the purposes of Addictions Counseling, this 'God' is of the client's *own conception*. If the therapist truly comprehends this idea, then it will become clear that it is *only* the *client's conception* of 'God' that is important in the therapeutic process. This is because as clients make *conscious contact* with the animating *power* within them, they are the only ones capable of appropriately *conceiving*, then becoming consciously aware of and actually *perceiving*, this powerful spiritual force – because it is theirs and theirs alone. It truly becomes a *personal relationship*.

The Goal of the Spiritual Counseling Approach

Total abstinence from addictions is the desired outcome or *goal* of the spiritual approach to counseling. This outcome is achieved through the client's gaining a conscious contact with his or her Creator. The obsession of the client's addiction is removed through attainment of that contact. An ongoing *daily* relationship of the client with this Creative Power keeps the client in a state of remission, and thus, free of addictive obsessions. It is the role of the counselor to guide clients in their quest to obtain and maintain this conscious contact with a Power Greater than themselves.

-----*******-----

The following sections are included to provide the counselor with a further source of background information with which to better assist their clients in coming to terms with *their own conception of a Power Greater than themselves.*

Law vs. Faith

Spirituality requires *faith,* and faith is 'the thing' that brings one into conscious contact with his or her Creator. In essence, *faith* is the dividing line between the secular-scientific methodology and the spiritual approach to recovery. From the religious perspective of a *Christian* worldview, this *faith* is the essential difference between Old Testament and New Testament covenant philosophies. Generally speaking, the Old Testament contains *The Commandments* and *The Law* or 'Torah' as revealed through Moses and the prophets. This philosophy believes that following Mosaic Law is what is necessary to gain favor with God. Generally, favor with God is measured *externally* by material possessions, societal esteem, etc. This is a cause and effect relationship. This *religious* principle does not necessarily require an internal faith, service to others, or attempts to feel that one had done their best to discover and follow the intent or spirit of the law. A personal relationship with God is not generally essential. All that is necessary is to follow the law. Neither is love of, or from, God an essential element. Forgiveness for not adhering to the law was granted not through contriteness, but through ritualistic material (animal) sacrifice. As such, the value system and redemptive power is *extrinsic,* or external, in nature. All that is required to gain acceptance and favor from God is to follow the law. Nothing else is required. Atonement for sin is through external material sacrifice as prescribed in Mosaic Law. Rewards and punishments (cause and effect) are dispersed in proportion to obedience to God's laws.

31

The New Testament philosophy, on the other hand, does not necessarily require strict adherence to prescribed 'laws,' but rather a requirement to "Love God, and love your neighbor as yourself." It was soon discovered that these commandments to *love* God, self, and others, required adherence to *moral* principles, and also to possess a humble *faith* and internal *sacrifice.* However, the sacrifice was not of a material nature, but of *self* - of selfish ends and selfish ideologies (What's in it for me?). The *reward* for *faith* is internal or *intrinsic.* It brings the believer into close, conscious, contact with his or her Creator. This contact invites a relationship in which the believer gains forgiveness, acceptance, self-discipline, and love. Love, that God always wishes to share; Love which is accepted *through faith* as received. And *love,* when returned back to God, is often returned in a manner that also flows to others through self-sacrifice and service.

This spiritual connectedness has few conditions and has been observed to possess immense restorative powers. The book "Alcoholics Anonymous" informs the reader that there are wide variations in how each individual "approaches and conceives of the [Spiritual] Power which is greater than self." Whether or not one agrees with a particular approach seems to make little difference in the outcome of the process. The point is that each individual finds an approach that works for them. The book "Alcoholics Anonymous" states:

"On one proposition, however, these men and women are strikingly agreed. Every one of them has gained access to, and believes in, a Power greater than himself. This Power has in each case accomplished the miraculous, the humanly impossible." "Here are thousands of men and women, worldly indeed. They flatly declare that since they have come to believe in a Power greater than themselves, to take a certain attitude toward that

32

Power, and to do certain simple things, there has been a revolutionary change in their way of living and thinking. In the face of collapse and despair, in the face of the total failure of their human resources, they found that a new power, peace, happiness, and sense of direction flowed into them. This happened soon after they wholeheartedly met a few simple requirements. Once confused and baffled by the seeming futility of existence, they show the underlying reasons why they were making heavy going of life. Leaving aside the drink question, they tell why living was so unsatisfactory. They show how *the change* came over them. When many hundreds of people are able to say that the *consciousness* of the Presence of God is today the most important fact of their lives, they present a powerful reason why one should have *faith*." (*emphasis* added) (Anonymous, 2001, pp. 50-51).

There too is a cause and effect relationship of sorts, but unlike old covenant law, the believer often feels as though the rewards received are vastly greater than those deserved. The believer may feel that he or she has committed unforgivable acts and omissions and are deserving of only punishment and despair. Yet, from the pit of damnation they often feel they have been lifted to great heights and rewarded beyond their wildest imaginings.

"Many of us have experienced dad's elation. We have indulged in spiritual intoxication. Like a gaunt prospector, belt drawn in over the last ounce of food, our pick struck gold. Joy at our release from a lifetime of frustration knew no bounds. Father feels he has struck something better than gold. For a time he may try to hug the new treasure to himself. He may not see at once that he has barely scratched a limitless lode which will pay dividends only if he mines it for the rest of his life and insists on giving away the entire product." (Anonymous, 2001, pp. 128-129).

Extrinsic vs. Intrinsic
(Secular-Scientific vs. Spiritual)

The above analogy of the 'prospector' is only made as an example for comparison to the spiritual counseling approach and the secular-scientific view. Apparently, the secular-scientific model, by its nature, can only intervene with 'rule-following,' cause and effect, methodologies. Of course, such mental health interventions also entail the use of therapies designed to discover possible internal deficiencies that may have produced conditions under which certain addictions were spawned. Regardless of the cause, secular non-spiritual recovery requires that rules be followed and *external* sacrifices be made. Theoretically, if the client follows the rules, the addiction or addictive behavior should stop or be diminished.

However, once remission of the addictive behavior has occurred, *feelings return,* and clients are left only with: 1) self, 2) the therapist, 3) rules, and 4) the raw emotions that were once soothed by indulgence in their addiction. The counselor–client relationship then centers on what can be done to help the client alleviate residual feelings of emptiness, hopelessness, unworthiness, injustice, and other emotional, and often physical symptoms. It is at this stage where the secular-scientific approach to therapy regularly fails because it provides no effective ongoing relief of symptoms for the addiction. Additionally, this is the juncture in the therapeutic process at which the goals of secular-scientific therapy are deemed to have been met. Thus, it is at this point where remuneration for counseling services ends and therapy is terminated. Typically, without continued therapeutic support, relapse soon follows.

The spiritual approach however, attempts to bring the client to a point of involvement, and into a relationship with, a Power greater than him or herself. This relationship requires *faith,* and faith *lived* requires *action.* The action taken by the client, under the guidance of this newfound Power, lifts the client 'out-of-self' by being of service to others. As this process occurs, obsessions and addictions tend to diminish and are replaced by feelings of usefulness and fulfillment. These 'feelings' are later found to be a *reward* of the process, and upon these positive feelings a life filled with love, joy, peace, and happiness can be built. Material rewards may come, but such are not the intended consequence of the spiritual therapeutic process. Instead, they are the result of an altered attitude and increased motivation to become a more productive and contributing member of society, and to be of greater service to their fellows ("mining for the rest of [one's] life and giving away the entire product").

If the Universe were to be viewed statistically, and the question were posed: "What is the probability that all of 'this' happened by chance?" The answer, and resultant statistical outcome, would approach "zero." This same response is typically received when alcoholics and those with other addictions, who have experienced a spiritual contact with their Creator, and through this contact have then witnessed miraculous occurrences in their own lives - that no *human* remedy had been able to produce - are asked: "What is the probability that these life altering events happened by chance?"

There is no evidentiary cause for either of these miraculous events to have happened by chance. In fact, the odds against the chance occurrences of the Universe coming into existence on its own, and some of the chains-of-events that have occurred to bring those with addictions into a conscious contact with their Creator, are monumentally high. Yet, despite knowledge of the occurrence of these miraculous events, science typically rejects the notion of *spiritual* healing in the lives of humankind. *Science* rejects the observable events of successful spiritual interventions in that they do not lend themselves to being quantified, measured, predicted, or replicated through current scientific methods.

At one time science believed that the reports of miraculous spiritual interventions were merely the effects produced by *placebos* and/or *nocebos*. The physical and mental 'effects' produced by these phenomena are generated through the use of *suggestive* powers. As such, science once believed and explained that the seemingly miraculous recoveries and events claimed by some as attributable to spiritual interventions and experiences, were actually just effects produced by the power of suggestion to vulnerable or predisposed clients. However, individuals who are severely addicted are not typically susceptible to placebos or other suggestive or imaginary forces. As will be discussed later, the *power* necessary for alcoholics, and those otherwise seriously addicted, to be successful in their struggle to overcome their addictions, must be derived from a source that is more powerful than their addiction.

This book attempts to examine the nature and scope of *spirituality* as it pertains to addictions counseling. The psychiatric and counseling professions and today's society in general, for varied reasons, tend to take a jaundiced view of all things *spiritual*. This perception was described in a recent article on the topic where it was stated that: "In some ways, spirituality and religion have together become the "third rail" of the mental health field: clinicians may think these topics are so highly charged that they keep their distance and avoid talking with patients about their spiritual or religious beliefs." (Harvard Medical School, 10-2007). As such, spiritual concepts, practices, and beliefs are not broached in the majority of contemporary psychology and counseling educational training programs. The educational programs that do provide training in the transcendent philosophies are typically geared toward a particular religious or biblical approach. Consequently, a professional divide exists between therapists who take a strict secular-scientific approach and those who take a scientific yet religious approach. Interestingly, neither of these seemingly polar counseling philosophic approaches has achieved the significant and lasting results produced by administration of the spiritual approach as first delineated in the program of Alcoholics Anonymous.

With Sobriety,
All Else
Is Possible

Chapter 6

'Spirituality' and 'Spiritual Conception' Defined

Definition of *Spiritual*: "of, relating to, consisting of, or affecting the spirit; incorporeal (spiritual needs); of or relating to sacred matters; ecclesiastical rather than lay or temporal (spiritual authority); concerned with religious values; related or joined in spirit; of or relating to supernatural beings or phenomena; of, relating to, or involving spiritualism; spiritualistic" (Merriam-Webster, 1999). In this book the term *Spirituality* is based on the definition of its root word 'Spirit.' The word spirituality has taken on many different connotations and is often a confusing term to grasp. This book is centered on the spiritual aspect of the addictions recovery process. The book "Alcoholics Anonymous" is used as a primary reference in this investigation as it is essentially the founding document that established a working, spiritually based, 12 Step recovery program. All other such addiction recovery programs utilize the effective and proven principles outlined in the A.A. book.

The term *Spirituality* tends to be used interchangeably with the word and concept of *God* in the book "Alcoholics Anonymous." As previously discussed, current day secular psychological therapeutic methodologies utilize counseling programs based on the scientific method. Christian or Biblical based addiction counseling methods are based on specific Christian teachings, and Biblical principles and concepts. Both of these methods require adherence to their

39

foundational precepts. The foundational precepts of the program of Alcoholics Anonymous are *suggestive* in nature, and generally *non-directive* as to how results are to be achieved. However, when attained, the results are commonly universal. This examination then looks at the definition of spirituality from the non-definitive, Alcoholics Anonymous perspective.

From "Bill's Story" in the book "Alcoholic Anonymous:"

> "The word God still aroused a certain antipathy. When the thought was expressed that there might be a God personal to me this feeling was intensified. I didn't like the idea. I could go for such conceptions as Creative Intelligence, Universal Mind or Spirit of Nature but I resisted the thought of a Czar of the Heavens, however loving His sway might be. I have since talked with scores of men who felt the same way. My friend suggested what then seemed a novel idea. He said, "*Why don't you choose your own conception of God?*" That statement hit me hard. It melted the icy intellectual mountain in whose shadow I had lived and shivered many years. I stood in the sunlight at last. *It was only a matter of being willing to believe in a Power greater than myself. Nothing more was required of me to make my beginning.* I saw that growth could start from that point." (Anonymous, 2001, p. 12)

This quotation indicates a concept of a Higher Spiritual Power that can be unique and personal to the client and not dependent on any particular religion, sect, or denomination.

Steps 11 and 12 are also instructive in formulating an individual concept of this 'God,' a personal contact with this 'God,' and the spiritual experience resulting from a faithful taking of these steps:

"11. Sought through prayer and meditation to improve our conscious contact with God *as we understood Him*, praying only for knowledge of His will for us and the power to carry that out."

"12. Having had a spiritual awakening as the result of these steps, we tried to carry this message to alcoholics, and to practice these principles in all our affairs."
(Anonymous, 2001, pp. 59-60).

In these steps the terms "God" and "Spirituality" are used in similar contexts and representative of one conceptual entity. Again, no particular religion or denomination is delineated or promoted. Nor does Alcoholics Anonymous attempt to set itself apart as its own religion, sect, or denomination. Neither does Alcoholics Anonymous attempt to countermand the secular-scientific or religious approaches, or the medical view. The concept of "God," or "Spirit," or "Power Greater than self" is defined by the individual client and is unique to them. The only stipulation for the client's personal growth in recovery is that they do have *a* "Higher Power" and that it must be something that they perceive as a "Power Greater than Themselves." Obviously then too, clients cannot be their own "Higher Power."

A.A.'s Relationship with the Medical and Religious Community

In addition to not representing any particular religious, medical, or scientific point of view, Alcoholics Anonymous actually assists and encourages these and other viewpoints and concepts. This *spiritual* attitude taken by the early A.A. membership not only established cordial relations with the medical and religious communities, it established lasting friendships. As such, Alcoholics

Anonymous has been welcomed by the medical and religious communities and has also been sought after when these very same institutions found it necessary to seek assistance in matters related to addictions recovery. Thus, doors were opened for broad cooperation, growth, mutual understanding, and acceptance for all.

"Alcoholics Anonymous is not a religious organization. Neither does A.A. take any particular medical point of view, though we cooperate widely with the men of medicine as well as with the men of religion. Alcohol being no respecter of persons, we are an accurate cross section of America, and in distant lands…. By personal religious affiliation, we include Catholics, Protestants, Jews, Hindus, …. Moslems, and Buddhists."

"Another reason for the wide acceptance of A.A. was the ministration of friends - friends in medicine, religion, and the press, together with innumerable others who became our able and persistent advocates." (Anonymous, 2001, p. xx).

'Spirit' and 'Spirituality' Defined

As indicated, an explanation of the "spiritual concept" employed by Alcoholics Anonymous is somewhat elusive. One knows if/when *It* is 'present,' but *Its* presence is difficult to define. From a dictionary perspective *"Spirit,"* as connoted in A.A. is defined as: The source of *animation* or vital core empowered to bring forth life to the mind and body; A supernatural being or essence that (for A.A. purposes) is representative of "good" such as a Holy Spirit; An eternal Soul; A bodiless, invisible essence of *being* that is capable of entering and altering a human mind, heart, and body; The intelligent, emotional, or sentient portion of a person that transcends flesh and bone; A supernatural change-agent only perceived by the individual.

Alcohol itself has also been defined as a *'Spirit'* or of containing 'spirits.' The origin of the term 'Spirit' is from Middle English, from Anglo-French or Latin; Anglo-French, espirit, spirit, from Latin spiritus, literally, *'breath,'* from spirare to blow, or to breathe. Its first known use was in the 13th century. Its Synonyms are *psyche* and/or *soul*. (Merriam-Webster, 1999)

These definitions are still lacking in the overall Alcoholics Anonymous connotation. In the A.A. sense it would be more accurate to describe the *Spirit* as: "The *Life Giving Universal Force, God, Creator, or Essence* whose nature is *"Spirit."* The definition of spirit as "Breath" presents a picture of one who has been breathed upon by, or received breath from, a Universal Creator, and through which has received life or animation. One who is no longer just a sum total of parts, but one whose parts have been brought to life through a *Spiritual power*. The essence of this life giving *Spirit*, or *Animating Force*, then is *'in'* all of humankind and is thusly the same essential force that is contained in the universal *'God/Spirit.'* Although this force is certainly contained in all living things, humankind possesses a greater access to a higher order of this essence of 'God' than other living things, in that, humankind has the ability to feel emotion and possesses the intellectual power to think, reason, *choose,* and *act* based not only on instinct, but on *'free-will.'*

Finding "God"

This higher ordered animating force or concept of 'God,' that is believed to be in all of us, is typically pushed aside, buried, and prejudiciously ignored in the egocentric, self-absorbed, addicted individual. However, the powerful essence of the 'Spirit' or 'God' is apparently ever-present. Clients may speculate that 'God' has abandoned them, or turned His back on them when in fact, it is the

43

clients who have typically turned their back on 'God.' As such, 'God' has not forsaken the client, nor is 'God' lost. In most cases, all the client needs to do to *'find'* 'God' is to - figuratively and emotionally, - *turn around*. If one is seeking to *find* 'God' we can rest assured that 'God' is not the one who is lost.

"Yet we had been seeing another kind of flight, a spiritual liberation from this world, people who rose above their problems. They said God made these things possible, and we only smiled. We had seen spiritual release, but liked to tell ourselves it wasn't true. Actually we were fooling ourselves, for deep down in every man, woman, and child, is the fundamental idea of God. It may be obscured by calamity, by pomp, by worship of other things, but in some form or other it is there. For faith in a Power greater than ourselves, and miraculous demonstrations of that power in human lives, are facts as old as man himself. We finally saw that faith in some kind of God was a part of our make-up, just as much as the feeling we have for a friend. Sometimes we had to search fearlessly, but He was there. He was as much a fact as we were. We found the Great Reality deep down within us. In the last analysis it is only there that He may be found. It was so with us." (Anonymous, 2001, p. 55).

With Sobriety,
All Else
Is Possible

Chapter 7

Awakening to Spiritual Concepts

The Universal Prayer of the Hopeless Alcoholic or Addict

A common thread that runs through the personal stories of recovered alcoholics, and those with other addictions, is the apparent power of a particular prayer; a prayer that most of them have unwittingly voiced just prior to commencing the spiritual journey of recovery. This prayer is typically uttered when in the state of absolute despair. This nearly universal simple prayer is unconditional in nature. Its words may vary somewhat, but is usually made while alone and in a state of absolute unreserved desperation. The prayer is: *"God help me."*

This prayer is not expressed for the purpose of the acceptance of a religion or even an acceptance of, or a belief in, 'God,' but more as a final act of sheer desperation. Following utterance of this prayer, most personal stories continue with amazing accounts of a series of seemingly unrelated coincidental events that lead them to profound alterations in the courses of their lives. At first glance these events appear to be chance occurrences, but later it is realized that the probability of such events occurring by chance is so small that they fall within the realm of the *miraculous*. Initially, these events might be viewed as *coincidental*. However, after witnessing countless similar occurrences, the definition of the word "coincidence" can no longer be used as an explanation to credibly define these repeated life-altering events. Later, if addicted individuals commence exploration of a 12 Step program, they will begin investigation of spiritual concepts unique to themselves. As such, they will start to formulate their own connection to a "Higher Power," or 'God.' The book "Alcoholics Anonymous" describes how numerous members were initially repulsed by talk of spiritual matters and how such feelings were addressed:

"As soon as a man can say that he does believe, or is willing to believe, we emphatically assure him that he is on his way. It has been repeatedly proven among us that upon this simple cornerstone a wonderfully effective spiritual structure can be built... That was great news to us, for we had assumed we could not make use of spiritual principles unless we accepted many things on faith which seemed difficult to believe... When people presented us with spiritual approaches, how frequently did we all say... I cannot accept as surely true the many articles of faith which are so plain to [others]. So it was comforting to learn that we could commence at a simpler level."

"Besides a seeming inability to accept much on faith, we often found ourselves handicapped by obstinacy, sensitiveness, and unreasoning prejudice. Many of us have been so touchy that even casual reference to spiritual things made us bristle with antagonism... Though some of us resisted, we found no great difficulty in casting aside such feelings. *Faced with alcoholic destruction, we soon became as open minded on spiritual matters as we had tried to be on other questions. In this respect alcohol was a great persuader. It finally beat us into a state of reasonableness."* (emphasis added) (Anonymous, 2001, pp. 47-48).

'Change' based on Spiritual Experience

A *spiritual awakening* comes when the addicted individual seeks the assistance of 'God' and becomes *willing* to receive spiritual help. This willingness starts the chain of events that may lead to the client coming into conscious contact with 'God.' This conscious contact with the Creator has been likened to two raindrops on a windowpane. At the slightest touch, one to another, they merge and become 'one.' A similar merging of *spirits* is the essence of *spiritual experience*. It may bring about an immediate change in how the client reacts to the world's events and situations. This merging of the internal spirit may also explain the feelings of camaraderie often described by members of recovery fellowships. Instantly upon contact, these individuals appear to relate positively, one-to-the-other, anywhere in the world, regardless of social standing, race, creed, color, religion, etc. Initially, they define themselves as "people who would not mix," but they describe a 'spiritual magic' that occurs when people, who are in conscious contact with their own Higher Power, come together and share of themselves. "We are people who normally would not mix. But there exists among us a fellowship, a friendliness, and an understanding which is indescribably wonderful." (Anonymous, 2001, p. 17).

This spiritual *merging* with 'God' often generates a strong feeling of closeness and unity. To some, this feeling of closeness to 'God' comes quickly, like a raindrop (self) into the ocean (God). But to others it's been known to grow more slowly over time, like a raindrop to puddle, to stream, to river, and finally home to the ocean. This is not uncommon and can often be beneficial to the client. The simple fact that the client is "on the journey" initiates internal *change*. This internal *'transformation'* soon produces outward displays of alterations in behaviors, feelings, attitudes, and outlook.

More often than not, these *changes* are noticed by family, friends, co-workers, etc. long before the client is aware of them.

Skeptical clients will want to know what it will feel like after they take spiritual steps - before taking them. However, discussions concerning the results of taking spiritual actions, and of subsequent thoughts and feelings, are typically fruitless. One cannot know how something will *feel* that hasn't yet been *experienced*. Nevertheless, driven by fear of relapse and by carefully observing what 'living by spiritual principles' has achieved in the lives of others, the client usually 'comes to believe' that recovery, gained through practicing spiritual principles, is available to them as well. Science teaches that results must be *seen* to be *believed*. Inversely however, in the realm of spiritually based addictions recovery, it becomes apparent that some things must first be *believed*, before they can be *seen*.

> "Seemingly he could not drink even if he would. God had restored his sanity. What is this but a miracle of healing? Yet its elements are simple. Circumstances made him willing to believe. He humbly offered himself to his Maker - *then he knew*. Even so has God restored us all to our right minds. To this man, the revelation was sudden. Some of us grow into it more slowly. But He has come to all who have honestly sought Him. When we drew near to Him He disclosed Himself to us!" (*emphasis* added) (Anonymous, 2001, p. 57).

A *spiritual awakening* then, can come as a sudden emotional and spiritual upheaval or, with its foundation laid; it can grow slowly over time. However, regardless of how *it* occurs, *its* effects cannot be comprehended *prior* to *its* occurrence. The experience of having a conscious contact with 'God' cannot be understood until such a contact is sought and *experienced*. Such an experience then does not lend itself easily to secular-scientific analysis. Casual observers or participants in a typical 'experimental group' cannot simply follow a set of external instructions and consistently be led to have a spiritual experience. Although a spiritual experience may occur in such individuals, the experience would not be based on the experimental scientific instructions administered. A spiritual experience is a one-on-one consummation of a personal relationship with one's own conception of a Power Greater than self, i.e., 'God.'

Many alcoholics, and those with other addictive disorders, arrive at this *decision point* in the recovery process with great distrust for all things human. Additionally, they often feel unwanted, unloved, and/or undeserving of a personal connection to 'God.' They fear ridicule and rejection. They distrust what they are told by counselors and others, and they distrust and/or disbelieve their current conception of 'God.' Thus, this experiential concept presents great difficulty to those who feel they must be able to *reason* their way through the process and obtain a concept of what a spiritual experience would be like *prior* to actually committing to the suggested actions necessary to potentially have such an experience. They wish to adhere to the scientific model that "things must be *seen* to be *believed*." They have difficulty with the faith concept of *believing* prior to *seeing* the results. A common phrase that may now take on new meaning to them and may help such clients is: "I was blind, but now I see." (NAB, 1992, p. Jn 9:25).

Most individual clients in a typical non-addictions oriented counseling situation, would be unwilling to discuss such a spiritual step much less take one. However, clients in the hopeless stages of alcoholism and/or other addictions are often in a life-and-death undertaking. As such, they are much more likely to *believe* that there is a solution, and be more *willing* to take a *blind* step of *faith*, in order to *see*. In these situations there is virtually nowhere else to go. All other alternatives have failed. The all-or-nothing last desperate act of those in the grip of a hopeless addiction is: "God help me!"

Willingness (the Key), Faith, Decision, and Action

When clients come in contact with others who have suffered the same hopelessness and addictions they have experienced; Yet, these others appear to have actually recovered from their condition on the basis of having had a *spiritual experience*; Then, although skeptical, clients may start to become open to the possibility of at least being *willing* to believe. Certainly *reason* is not to be discouraged or left out of this process, as it plays a prominent role. A spiritual experience is not something that is entered into lightly or without considerable thought. The book "Alcoholics Anonymous" relates that *reason* will bring one to the decision point regarding the concept of 'God.' It states: "God is either everything or else He is nothing. God either is, or He isn't." The book indicates that *reason* will only bring a client so far toward acceptance of, and a relationship with, 'God;' *Faith* will be required to complete the journey. An example of one such experience was told as:

> "Some of us had already walked far over the Bridge of Reason toward the desired shore of faith... We were grateful that Reason had brought us so far. But somehow, we couldn't quite step ashore..." "One night, when confined in a hospital, he was approached by an alcoholic who had known a spiritual experience. Our friend's gorge rose as he bitterly cried out: "If there is a God, He certainly hasn't done anything for me!" But later, alone in his room, he asked himself this question: "Is it possible that all the religious people I have known are wrong?"

While pondering the answer he felt as though he lived in hell. Then, like a thunderbolt, a great thought came. It crowded out all else:

"Who are you to say there is no God?" This man recounts that he tumbled out of bed to his knees. In a few seconds he was overwhelmed by a conviction of the Presence of God. It poured over and through him with the certainty and majesty of a great tide at flood. The barriers he had built through the years were swept away. He stood in the Presence of Infinite Power and Love. He had stepped from bridge to shore. For the first time, he lived in conscious companionship with his Creator. Thus was our friend's cornerstone fixed in place. No later vicissitude has shaken it. His alcoholic problem was taken away." (Anonymous, 2001, pp. 53,56)

Thus, *reason* is seen as bringing one to a decision point, yet a leap of *faith* is required once the *willingness* to believe, or the decision to believe, is made. Some individuals have reported that after having made this leap of faith, "A new world came into view," or that they felt as though they were "Rocketed into the fourth dimension of existence." Others have stated that they felt nothing, but later, after some period of sobriety, or cessation of their addiction, they "looked back" and the realization that the probability of them progressing to their current position in life, in comparison to where they had come from, was truly miraculous. In this realization that they, in and of themselves, could not have made such progress, report becoming awash in the feeling of the Presence of 'God.' (Anonymous, 2001, pp. 12, 25, 100).

For clients new in the process of recovery, the spiritual concept may be daunting. However, they should understand that the 'God' they are to develop a relationship with, and the 'Spirit' they are to come into contact with, are those of their own conception. Neither the counselor nor anyone else in any *official* 12 Step recovery program will dictate who 'God' is for them. Of particular note too, is that the client need not even actually *believe* in their conception of 'God' or the *Spirit*, only that they become *willing* to commence the process to do so. Once they become *willing* to commence the spiritual journey, *the journey begins*. Once the journey begins, it starts to take on a life of its own. A life that is personal to the client. Thus, as noted in a 'saying' of 12 Step programs: "*Willingness* is the *key*."

With Sobriety,
All Else
Is Possible

Chapter 8

Counseling Concepts of: "Location," "Call," and "Silent Contemplation"

This counseling adaptation has been influenced by the concepts for Christian Counseling delineated in the work of Ian Jones "The Counsel of Heaven on Earth: Foundations for Biblical Christian Counseling" (Jones, 2006). Although there are fundamental differences between Christian counseling and counseling based on spiritual principles - directed toward spiritual *awareness* - the simple and basic Biblical approach outlined by Dr. Jones can be easily adapted to the spiritual approach of addictions counseling. Dr. Jones utilizes the messages contained in the beginning and at the end of the Bible to bring into focus the central theme of, and basis for, Bible based, Christian oriented, non-secular counseling.

All counselors receive years of training and internship whereby they are taught numerous psychological counseling philosophies and techniques. These techniques involve every aspect of the counseling situation including seating arrangements, setting, environment, tone, rapport building, style, approach, phraseology, etc., etc. All of these issues are good and necessary for successful therapy. However, from a spiritual perspective, they typically leave out the most important aspects of counseling. Those aspects include: a source of Power, an appropriate starting place, and the ultimate purpose or goal for therapy.

Location

For Christian Counseling, Dr. Jones indicates that regardless of the counselor's technique or approach, counseling needs to begin with the client's relationship with God. To illustrate this point he uses Genesis chapter 3. Genesis chapter 3 details the "Fall of Man" from grace with God, in that *man*, Adam, disobeyed God and ate from the "Tree of Life and Knowledge of Good and Evil." After eating of the fruit, Adam's eyes were opened and he realized that he had 'chosen' to violate the rule that God had asked him to obey. When God returned to the Garden, Adam covered himself and hid from God. Since, as discussed previously, God foreknows all things, but is not responsible for all that He foreknows, God knew of Adam's choice and action but did not *choose* Adam's actions for him. God inquired then of Adam's honesty and spiritual condition, not because God didn't know, but because *Adam* needed to know. So, rather than invading Adam's hiding place and informing Adam that He knew of his transgressions, God called out to Adam and asked instead: *"Where are you?"* (NAB, 1992, Gen 3:9).

The client's answer to the question: "Where are you?" provides addictions counselors with initial information regarding the client's starting point for treatment. As with Adam, the answer to this one question will establish for the counselor and the client: 1) *Where* the client stands in their relationship with 'God,' and thus; 2) The *direction* and *distance* the counseling process needs to move in order to reach the ultimate destination/goal of the therapeutic process; ie., the client's return to harmony with 'God.' The client's response to this question will guide the follow-on therapeutic process. This process will help the client begin the procedure of determining: 1) The identity of the 'God' of their own conception (who); 2) Where they are in relationship to their 'God' (direction); 3) What steps are necessary in order to draw closer to 'God' (distance); and 4) What type of life-altering changes will the client need to make as he or she draws near to the goal of atonement and coming into harmony with 'God.' The client's response to the question: *"Where are you?"* is the beginning of the therapeutic plan that starts the process of recovery.

Secrets

In a further examination of the "Eden" story, Adam, in order to reduce his own guilt and anxiety, and in an attempt to diminish personal responsibility for his own actions, blamed his disobedience on the "woman," Eve. As such, Adam further separated himself from God. Adam knew that he was responsible for his own disobedience and that he was guilty of not protecting Eve from the intimidation and manipulative influence of the Serpent. This writer speculates that, in an attempt to lessen the severity of God's displeasure in him, Adam felt he needed to lie to, and keep secrets from, God; Secrets of deception and omission, of things done and not done. A saying relevant to this situation often utilized in 12 Step programs is: "You are only as sick as your secrets." Secrets tend to separate one from God. Secrets create anxiety. Secrets create the necessity for people to feel the need to hide for fear of discovery. Holding secrets begins the process of mental, emotional, and physical decay. Thus, keeping secrets begins the downward spiral into spiritual sickness.

Addictions usually mask the destructive feelings produced by this type of emotional decay and spiritual disease. Thus, abstinence from addictions often lays bare serious issues. However, those issues usually cannot be addressed when addictions are active. As such, when abstinence is achieved, significant and substantive work must be done to remediate the client's underlying spiritual and emotional difficulties. If not, relapse is virtually assured. The "Steps" in Alcoholics Anonymous, and subsequent 12 Step programs, are a proven tool to assist in the alleviation of these significant underlying issues. Counselors, of course, will want to start the process of assisting the client in purging themselves of emotional baggage. However, this recovery process is life-long - as are their addictions. As such, ongoing therapeutic assistance is warranted. Such assistance may include: continued individual therapy; various types of group counseling; and/or involvement in support groups - 12 Step or otherwise. Whatever form of continuing care is decided upon, it should provide frequent, on-going, and consistent support. Again, addictions may be placed in remission, but they are *not cured*. As such, continuing support is strongly recommended.

The Call

Dr. Jones also references God's words, as noted from the end of the final book of the Bible. These words, which essentially close both the book of Revelation and the Bible, are in the form of an invitation or a "call" to all people: "The Spirit and the bride say "Come." Let the hearer say "Come." Let the one who thirsts come forward, and the one who wants it receive the gift of life-giving water." (NAB, 2002 Rev 22:17).

In a Christian counseling sense, Dr. Jones notes two principles of Biblical text to represent a "Location" and a "Call." These two basic elements of Christian counseling appear simplistic, but are vitally important to the process. These elements also present an excellent representation of the principle components of the spiritually based approach to counseling. As noted previously, the client first determines his or her *location* in relation to 'God' and then, if the client *listens*, he or she receives an *invitation* from 'God' to "*Come.*"

This 'Call' or *invitation,* emanating from the client's own conception of 'God,' may prove to be a vital and emotional step. This 'God' is not imaginary. Willingness opens the door. 'God' then enters and molds the client's conception of 'Him.' It should be noted that, at this point, clients may not yet have fully come to terms with this 'God' of their own conception. This need not be a hindrance, as long as clients are *willing* to believe that there is a *Power* in the universe that is greater than themselves and their addictions. Regardless, the emotional impact that clients may feel from this *invitation* can be overwhelming. Typically, clients with addictions often feel abandoned, ostracized, unworthy, inferior, undeserving, etc. Then, when they hear *God's Call*, inviting them to *"Come,"* they may experience an overwhelming feeling of finally being loved, wanted, and accepted by 'God.' Such a feeling is often referred to as a "spiritual experience." When the invitation to *"Come"* is heard, the counseling process shifts from one of seeking 'God' to one of moving toward this newly discovered 'God' of the client's own conception. This will bring the client into alignment and conscious contact with this previously inconceivable 'God.' (Jones, 2006).

Silent Contemplation

A philosophical process similar to 'Call' and 'Location' is *Silent Contemplation.* One method of silent contemplation is referred to as *Centering Prayer.* In his book "Intimacy with God" Thomas Keating wrote that: "Centering Prayer is an acceptance not only of God's *presence,* but also of God's *action.* Our experience during a period of prayer (or even outside of it) needs to be understood in the context of our relationship to the Spirit, which is primarily therapeutic. Why? Because we are sick!" This *centering* or *contemplative* state is also another form of ascertaining one's *location,* or an understanding of the seeker's "relationship to the Spirit." A similar reference is made in Step 11 of the book "Alcoholics Anonymous": "Sought through prayer and meditation to improve our conscious contact with God *as we understood Him*, praying only for knowledge of His will for us and the power to carry that out." (Anonymous, 2001, p. 59). Those suffering from addictions, who seek solace from 'God,' desire of Him: closeness, guidance, and power. The power they seek is not for themselves, but for use in the service of others, and in bringing the seeker closer to 'God.'

Thomas Keating further discussed the *language* of contact with God. He relates that: "St. John of the Cross wrote, "The Father spoke one word from all eternity and he spoke it in silence, and it is in silence that we hear it." This suggests that *silence* is God's first language and that all other languages are poor translations." (Keating, 1994). This silent reflection and contemplative outreach then would tend to open and fine-tune one's receptive listening in order to better perceive God's uncluttered, simplistic, communication to the innermost being of the one who listens and hears. This concept reflects the language of spiritual recovery which instructs one to be still, quiet, and to wait for intuitive insightfulness:

"…We may face indecision. We may not be able to determine which course to take. Here we ask God for inspiration, an intuitive thought or a decision. We relax and take it easy. We don't struggle. We are often surprised how the right answers come…" (Anonymous, 2001, p. 86).

Additionally, Psalms chapter 46 notes: "Be still and know that I am God." In the context in which it is used, this quotation notes that although the world around us is in turmoil and distress… "Be still, and know…" In this context, in silence and stillness, *answers* to lifelong dilemmas often quietly appear to the innermost self. Further, the intuitive awareness of 'God's' presence is the essential element of spiritual experience. Hence, the silent, wordless, interaction that occurs between 'God' and those who seek Him, produces the *feeling* of being emotionally touched by 'God.' This *feeling* is often described by those who have experienced it as "A silent communication, without words, that transfers to the 'hearer' an experiential knowledge of His presence, understanding, care, and love." (Keating, 1994).

In reality, these seemingly basic and simplistic concepts are very powerful tools. With these tools, if humbly and earnestly utilized, the client can commence a process whereby a spiritual relationship with one's Creator may be established. Establishment of a spiritual connectedness will assist in significantly improving the client's addiction driven mental obsessions and physical maladies. However, this remedy is restorative, but not curative. Remission of the client's symptoms is maintained by daily conscious contact with the client's "Higher Power" or "God." This spiritual condition may be maintained each day in the same way it was established, by: 1) Choosing to 'hear' 'God's' *call; 2)* By seeking to honestly determine one's *location* in relation to 'God;' 3) By taking actions that will move one closer to 'God;' and 4) By daily reflection with silent meditative and contemplative listening in order to *hear* 'God' when He speaks.

These suggested practices are very similar to A.A.'s Steps 10, 11, and 12. These Steps were designed to be taken daily in order to maintain the alcoholic's spiritual condition. These steps are:

"10) Continued to take personal inventory and when we were wrong promptly admitted it.

11) Sought through prayer and meditation to improve our conscious contact with God as we understood Him, praying only for knowledge of His will for us and the power to carry that out.

12) Having had a spiritual awakening as the result of these steps, we tried to carry this message to alcoholics, and to practice these principles in all our affairs."
(Anonymous, 2001, pp. 59-60).

With Sobriety,
All Else
Is Possible

Chapter 9

Counseling Toward a Spiritual Remedy

Abstinence

Unlike the objectives for other forms of counseling, for clients with addictive disorders, the ultimate goal of counseling is complete abstinence from the client's addiction. With the exception of appropriately prescribed medications that are taken as directed, included in the phrase *complete abstinence,* are *all* mood-altering chemical substances and addictive practices, irrespective of the client's current addiction. For example: the client cannot abstain from alcohol, but start smoking marijuana instead. Generally speaking, initially, all other issues are secondary to the client achieving entire abstinence. Entire abstinence is necessary due to the "phenomenon of craving" experienced by those with addictions. For many addictions, this *phenomenon of craving* is arrested during abstinence, but re-emerges if the client's addiction is indulged in, even briefly. Abstinence is necessary even with the understanding that the addiction may have initially been only a symptom of an underlying cause. Any attempts to discover this underlying *cause* will likely be fruitless unless the addiction is first remediated.

Though seemingly contrary to this notion of initial abstinence, the book "Alcoholics Anonymous" intimates that "causes and conditions" must be addressed if one's addiction is to be remediated.

Of course the A.A. book is correct in that assumption. However, it should be noted that when members of Alcoholics Anonymous begin the self-discovery process, they do so in a state of sobriety. To do so while intoxicated would prove pointless. "Our liquor was but a symptom. So we had to get down to causes and conditions. Therefore, we started upon a personal inventory. This was Step Four." In order for this process to come to a "successful consummation" the "Solution" offered necessitates "self-searching;" "leveling of pride;" "confession of shortcomings;" becoming teachable; picking up "the simple kit of spiritual tools laid at our feet;" and as a result, "we have had deep and effective spiritual experiences which have revolutionized our whole attitude toward life, toward our fellows, and toward God's universe." (Anonymous, 2001, pp. 64, 25).

It must be understood too, that *remediated* does not mean *healed*. Regardless of progress, a return to the addictive behavior will negate the therapeutic process and any previous gains are typically lost. As such, despite initial treatment and alleviation of symptoms, some form of long-term, on-going therapeutic involvement for the client will be necessary in order to prevent a relapse. To date, the most effective remedy for the alleviation of the majority of addictions is a spiritual one.

Why a Spiritual Remedy?

In order to remove the obsession that precedes the addictive behavior, why does a *spiritual remedy* or *spiritual experience* seem to be the necessary ingredient in Addictions Therapy? Why hasn't traditional counseling/therapy proven to be more effective? Although the answer to these questions is somewhat elusive to the secular therapist, a partial answer was gleaned from the recording of a speaker at a 1988 meeting of Alcoholics Anonymous. The speaker discussed his determination to seek the answer to why he had lingering feelings of despair, inadequacy, and suicidal ideations. He sought answers through various self-help organizations, counselors, hospitals, sanitariums, and other psychiatric institutions and therapeutic treatments. He stated that in each case he was given '*a*' diagnosis and '*an*' answer or reason for his internalized feelings. The speaker noted that although each of these diagnosis and answers differed, in their own way they were each valid for the symptoms presented, despite the fact that the presenting symptoms were the same in each clinical situation.

Nevertheless, although each diagnosis, from differing perspectives, brought him to *an* understanding of his issues, none of them offered him a viable *solution* that would alleviate his emotional difficulties. This speaker stated that after spending hundreds of hours in counseling and thousands of dollars for treatments, medications, and various types of therapies, the final result was that he: "…Wound up feeling crappy, and knowing why." (I, 1988). Knowing what his problems were and discussing his problems and his feelings with various therapists was informative, but these sessions did nothing to alleviate his addiction to alcohol.

It is evident then that the *solution* to addictions is not found in self-knowledge or in the 'knowing' of *why*. Knowing that there may be horrific issues in the client's background that produce debilitating emotional discomfort may appear to produce reasons for the client to engage in addictive behaviors, nevertheless, counseling the client in regard to these background issues typically does nothing to alleviate the client's addiction. These underlying issues though, often produce significant resentments. Resentments stand in the way of growth and recovery. From the book "Alcoholics Anonymous:"

"Resentment is the 'number one' offender. It destroys more alcoholics than anything else. From it stem all forms of *spiritual disease*, for we have been not only mentally and physically ill, we have been *spiritually sick*. When the *spiritual malady* is overcome, we straighten out mentally and physically."
(*Emphasis* added) (Anonymous, 2001, p. 64).

So then, the question that arises for the therapist is how to address the *spiritual* needs of the client in order that his or her other needs and conditions may be remediated as well.

Resentment and Spiritual Disease

"Highly competent psychiatrists who have dealt with us have found it sometimes impossible to persuade an alcoholic to discuss his situation without reserve." (Anonymous, 2001, p. 18).

The experience of Addictions Therapy is that deep resentment is not easily addressed through counseling practices that would normally prove effective. This is due to the spiritual bond between deep resentment and the 'soul' of the client. The roots of resentment enter into the central *being* of the client and create significant *disharmony*. Outwardly, resentment may seem to be only directed at others, but internal resentment of *self* infects the soul of the client as well. Thus, resentment produces a *spiritual* disease that is not readily treatable through non-spiritual means. This *disease-of-the-Spirit* then disassociates the client from the "Spirit of the Universe," or 'God.'

Deep seated resentments are not typically removed by ordinary 'talk' therapy. However, experientially, they have repeatedly been successfully removed through a "personality change" that is the result of an "awakening" to *spiritual principles*. This *awakening* has been sufficient to bring about recovery from addictions. Use of these principles was discovered in 1935 by the co-founders of Alcoholics Anonymous and has proven to be *an* effective method of assisting clients in the development of this *awakening*. (Anonymous, 2001, p. 567). However, each client is unique. As such, although the goal of obtaining a spiritual connectedness personal to the client remains the same, the path to the achievement of this objective is an individual one. Although the therapist can provide guidance, once the client achieves the willingness to commence the journey, the journey begins, and the outcome is tailored by the blossoming relationship between client and his or her Creator.

Although general therapeutic techniques are necessary and helpful in assisting with the counselor - client relationship, their use may have pitfalls and limitations when counseling a client with addictions. One potentially significant pitfall is a tendency for the counselor to be drawn into a *codependent* relationship with the client. Codependent tendencies in the counselor toward the client are an *intuitive* phenomenon, particularly in mental health professionals who are naturally empathetic and desire to be of maximum assistance to their clients. In Addictions Therapy, a counselor who succumbs to his or her codependent tendencies can spell disaster for both the client and the therapist. For all those who deal with alcoholics, and those with other addictions, the most effective attitude to take toward them is generally *counterintuitive* to those displayed in 'normal' situations with those who do not present with addictions. (O'Neal, 2011).

Additionally, normal therapeutic techniques, though helpful, are frequently ineffective in addictions counseling. As discussed earlier, they may provide *an* answer, but not a solution. In addictions counseling, therapeutic progress is not gained with *words*, but primarily through *action*. In Addictions Therapy, the *actions* that the client should be required to take, are often contrary to how he or she feels. In other words the client will be required to take certain prescribed *actions* before a change in thought, feeling, and attitude will occur. This counseling methodology, "Action Therapy," is currently beyond the scope of this book. However, as counselors and clients proceed and move through the therapeutic process, addictions counselors should understand the need for personal wariness against codependency, and a necessity to witness observable positive actions on the part of the client, as a measure of therapeutic progress.

Combating *spiritual disease* requires a *spiritual solution*. As for guiding the client toward a spiritual solution, the therapist should guide their client to a willingness to explore and expand their psyche – their *awareness*; the counselor should assist the client to come into a *state-of-being* whereby they are open to new ideas and concepts. A significant amount of client - counselor trust is necessary in order for clients with addictive disorders to permit themselves to be led into the realm of the *Spirit*. Spirituality may certainly be a new concept to some, but it is often an old and misunderstood concept to others. It is sometimes more difficult to clear out old ideas - particularly those of a punishing God - than it is to assist a client in looking into his or her heart in search of the *Spirit* within, or in seeking the conception of a loving 'God' personal to them.

This spiritual search may prove difficult. As such, the counselor may need to require *action* of the client in order to make spiritual progress. It is in the *doing* of things that clients will alter the course and pattern of their existence. This *opening* of self, and the *doing* of positive things, will then avail the seeker of the *power* of the *Spirit*. This *Power* cannot be seen or heard, but its restorative properties are evident for those who choose to become open to *It* and learn to *see* and *hear* - not *It* - but *evidence* of *Its* existence, by the recognizing of *Its* works.

So then, why hasn't traditional secular therapy proven to be more effective? For Addictions Therapy, secular-scientific counseling can offer *answers*, but *no solution*. Traditional secular-scientific psychoanalysis and therapy can determine the cause and nature of the client's underlying mental and emotional detriments. However, therapeutic work on the cause of the client's emotional distress will be of no effect if the client remains reliant on her or his addiction to soothe emotional symptoms. The counselor should understand that the client's addiction provides *immediate* relief of emotional pain. As such, unless the addiction is first remediated, and sustained sobriety and/or abstinence from other addictions is achieved, then there is little chance that traditional counseling or therapy will produce any positive improvement in any of the client's presenting areas of concern. Conversely, the spiritual approach - finding a Power greater than themselves, and more importantly, one that is greater than their addiction - has proven to greatly assist in not only the alleviation of the symptoms of addictive disorders, but in the remediation of other seemingly unrelated difficulties as well.

As soon as the addictive behaviors are in remission, which can often occur rapidly, then traditional secular-scientific therapy for other underlying psychological problems/issues may commence with reasonable assurance of success. Additionally, religious or Christian counselors may witness a hunger in their clients for greater knowledge of spiritual and religious concepts. Moreover, it is often discovered that once the addiction is in remission, many of the originally observed mental and physical difficulties no longer appear to be present. Nevertheless, those with addictions, who suffer from other disorders, are strongly encouraged to seek further assistance for those difficulties as necessity warrants (Anonymous, 2001, p. 133).

Non-Spiritual Recovery Model; An Example

Secular-science has attempted to emulate the spiritual therapeutic process without including the spiritual component. They have tried to get the results normally obtained through the spiritual approach while not actually using spiritual principles. This has been attempted through various experimental programs, philosophies, and techniques. For comparison purposes, to the Spiritual Model, one of the more prominent of such programs, the Transtheoretical Model of Behavior Change (DiClemente, 2004), involves moving the addicted client through Six Stages of "Change" to hopefully arrive at *abstinence*. Overall, each stage is proposed to take approximately six months to complete. At the end of each 6 month period the client should be prepared to move to the next stage or level of this program.

The Stages of the Transtheoretical Model are:
1) Precontemplation
2) Contemplation
3) Preparation
4) Action
5) Maintenance
6) Lapses and Learning.

These Stages entail therapeutic assistance in:
1) Thinking about abstinence;
2) Deeper thinking about why abstinence might be worthwhile;
3) Encouragement of the client to develop a plan to change his or her behavior;

4) Making a decision to put the plan into action and stop the addictive behaviors;

5) Join support groups and/or use on-going therapy to assist with situations that may cause temptation that may lead to a return to addictive behaviors (such situations might be office parties, etc.); and

6) A predicted return to old behavior and the resulting relapse into addictive behaviors.

Significant 'slips' [relapses] are built-in to the Transtheoretical Model and they often occur during the initial attempt at sobriety or abstinence. When these 'slips' occur, they are then attributed to a "flawed" action plan and the client returns to a lower stage. The client and therapist review their plan and processes, learn from mistakes, and start through the "stages" again. With this model, the client may eventually achieve abstinence from their addiction. However, since the client continued in their addiction throughout most of this transtheoretical process, much time has elapsed, and many counseling hours expended, with essentially no therapeutic progress made on the client's underlying causal factors.

The model in this process can be *enabling* to the client and may be open to significant manipulations. These manipulations by clients are calculated to ensure that they are able to remain in their addiction for as long as possible with minimal repercussions. Additionally, this model may induce codependent tendencies into the therapist (O'Neal, 2011). Moreover, since this model predicts relapse as a predetermined expectation, then all the client need do is fain an attempt at abstinence, followed by a significant preplanned relapse. The planned relapse will bring the client back to the initial stages of the Transtheoretical Model and guarantee continuing months or even years of accepted and excused indulgence in their addiction without consequence. Thus, the Transtheoretical Model may prove costly not only in terms of therapy expenses, but also in: lost time in sobriety, lost productivity/revenue, lost time with family, etc., often without successful recovery. Nevertheless, any acknowledgement on the part of the client, of the presence of an addictive disorder, and forward movement in pursuit of sobriety or abstinence, is a positive and well worthwhile endeavor.

If a Spiritual Solution is the Answer, are Healthcare Professionals Necessary?

If a spiritual remedy is the answer, and a spiritual manner of living is what is necessary to ensure continued abstinence and quality of life maintenance, then questions arise concerning the necessity for the use of doctors, counselors, psychologists, etc. If a spiritual experience is what is needed for recovery, why then are these healthcare professionals necessary? The book "Alcoholics Anonymous" describes and responds to such queries:

"A body badly burned by alcohol does not often recover overnight nor do twisted thinking and depression vanish in a twinkling. We are convinced that a spiritual mode of living is a most powerful health restorative. We, who have recovered from serious drinking, are miracles of mental health. But we have seen remarkable transformations in our bodies. Hardly one of our crowd now shows any mark of dissipation."

"But this does not mean that we disregard human health measures. God has abundantly supplied this world with fine doctors, psychologists, and practitioners of various kinds. Do not hesitate to take your health problems to such persons. Most of them give freely of themselves, that their fellows may enjoy sound minds and bodies. Try to remember that though God has wrought miracles among us, we should never belittle a good doctor or psychiatrist. Their services are often indispensable in treating a newcomer and in following his case afterward." (Anonymous, 2001, p. 133)

It must be understood that when discussing the writings of the book "Alcoholics Anonymous" the medical profession at the time was nearly entirely of the secular-scientific mindset. In 1939 when the book "Alcoholics Anonymous" was published, the spiritual realm of discussion was entirely left to clergy and supernaturalists. Although a few Doctors, such as Dr. Silkworth, who specialized in the treatment of alcoholics and drug addicts, would admit that they were having minimal success in treating their addicted patients, they also knew that some form of *Spiritual Remedy*, or *Moral Psychology,* was necessary. Dr. Silkworth states:

"We doctors have realized for a long time that some form of moral psychology was of urgent importance to alcoholics, but its application presented difficulties beyond our conception. What with our ultra-modern standards, our scientific approach to everything, we are perhaps not well equipped to apply the powers of good that lie outside our synthetic knowledge." "In nearly all cases, their [client's] ideals must be grounded in a power greater than themselves." "Psychiatrists," who despair from their ineffectiveness in working with alcoholics, "have accepted and encouraged this movement." "We feel, after many years of experience, that we have found *nothing* which has contributed more to the rehabilitation of these men than the altruistic movement now growing up among them." "...if a doctor is honest with himself, he must sometimes feel his own inadequacy. Although he gives all that is in him, it often is not

71

enough. One feels that something more than human power is needed to produce the essential psychic change... unless this person can experience an entire psychic change there is very little hope of his recovery." "...something more than human power is needed to produce the essential psychic change." (Anonymous, 2001, pp. xxvii-xxix).

Predating Alcoholics Anonymous, and perhaps one of the key individuals who set the stage for the founding principles of A.A., was the famous Psychiatrist Dr. Carl Jung. In 1930 Dr. Jung provided the best long-term therapy available to his patient Rowland H. Rowland was an alcoholic whose parents sent him to Dr. Jung to effect a cure for his alcoholism. However, within a very short time following a lengthy period of treatment, Rowland was drunk again. When Rowland returned to the doctor for further treatment, Dr. Jung refused re-admittance of him as a patient stating:

"You have the mind of a chronic alcoholic. I have never seen one single case recover, where that state of mind existed to the extent that it does in you." Our friend felt as though the gates of hell had closed on him with a clang.

He said to the doctor, "Is there no exception?"

"Yes," replied the doctor, "there is. Exceptions to cases such as yours have been occurring since early times. Here and there, once in a while, alcoholics have had what are called vital spiritual experiences. To me these occurrences are phenomena. They appear to be in the nature of huge emotional displacements and rearrangements. Ideas, emotions, and attitudes which were once the guiding forces of the lives of these men are suddenly cast to one side, and a completely new set of conceptions and motives begin to dominate them. In fact, I have been trying to produce some such emotional rearrangement within you. With many individuals the methods which I employed are successful, but I have never been successful with an alcoholic of your description."

Upon hearing this, our friend was somewhat relieved, for he reflected that, after all, he was a good church member. This hope, however, was destroyed by the doctor's telling him that while his religious convictions were very good, in his case they did not spell the necessary vital spiritual experience." (Anonymous, 2001, p. 27)

About 30 years later, after Alcoholics Anonymous was in full swing, Bill Wilson, co-founder of A.A., sent a letter to Dr. Jung inquiring of his experiences with Rowland H. Dr. Jung responded that he felt Rowland's craving for alcohol was "a search for wholeness" and an unfulfilled desire for "Union with God." Dr. Jung related to Bill:

"You see, "alcohol" in Latin is "spiritus" and you use the same word for the highest religious experience as well as for the most depraving poison. The helpful formula therefore is: spiritus contra spiritum." (Jung, 1961)

Although he was unable to produce the desired *psychic change*, or *spiritual experience,* in Rowland H., Dr. Jung recognized that in cases such as this, chronic alcoholism, a *spiritual* solution was necessary. Conversely, Dr. Jung's analysis points out that the *spirit* of alcohol severely weakens and may overcome man's internal *spirit*. Of their own devises, for chronic alcoholics, there is no recovery. Only the *Spirit* of 'God' is capable of overcoming the *Spirit* of alcohol. "Spiritus contra Spiritum." The literal translation is: Spirit against Spirit.

Today over 80 years have elapsed since the founding of the spiritually based program of recovery called Alcoholics Anonymous. Nevertheless, the debate still lingers in the secular-scientific/medical community: "Is there such a thing as spiritually based therapy? If so, does it work? If it does work, how?"

Recovery - The Goal of Spiritually Based Counseling

The goal of the spiritual approach to counseling is to assist the client to come into conscious contact with his or her Creator. If/when the client's internal spirit makes contact with the "God of his or her own conception," clients often feel as though they have become 'One' with their Creator. This "oneness" has been described as "being rocketed into a fourth dimension," a feeling of belonging, of fitting in, of finally finding one's place in the universe, of feeling *at home*, of "finding our Tribe," of being a part of God's Universe, of being a "child of God." (Anonymous, 2001, pp. 25, 336, 28). As the client begins the process of a spiritually induced healing, he or she begins the process of recovery. Addictions tend to take on a life of their own and often have drawn clients far from their 'normal' way of living. Though a relationship with their spiritual power often brings clients into a way of living that far exceeds expectations, the goal of "*Spirituality* in Addictions Counseling" is to return clients to their former state of being; to assist them to reclaim, to reacquire, to recoup, to regain, to repossess, to retake, to retrieve, to recapture, to get back to a manner of living that is not controlled by their addiction. From this starting point, new growth and new life begins.

Results such as these are not derived from a mere set of counseling techniques and discussions of pasts and issues, but rather by opening the therapeutic sessions to, and inviting into them, the presence of the *Spirit*, or the client's conception of 'God.' In so

74

doing, the *Spirit*, or 'God,' will invite the client – and therapist – to *"Come"* to Him. If the counselor and client are open to following directions and listening for, and being receptive to, *spiritual* revelations, they will discover a clear-cut, simple path for the client to follow to recovery. The term *recovery* does not just mean cessation of addictive behaviors. Recovery involves abstinence first, but then encompasses significant changes in lifestyle, outlook, and attitude. This recovery process will inevitably deviate from the counselor's original therapeutic plan. This deviation in the plan occurs as the *Spirit* begins to subtly gain directional authority over the counseling process. As this occurs, the client's embarked upon path will generally lead to the discovery of *where* the client *stands* in relation to the 'God' of his or her conception. (Jones, 2006). Once the client and counselor determine the client's *location* in relation to 'God,' the spiritual path necessary to move closer to Him, and thus recovery, will become readily apparent.

One working pathway toward this spiritual remedy is delineated in chapter 5 of the book "Alcoholics Anonymous" titled "How it Works" as: "Rarely have we seen a person fail who has thoroughly followed our path." This path leads to the 12 steps. The prerequisite to successful completion of the 12 steps is the *willingness* of clients to fully commit to the process and to possess the capacity to be "honest with themselves." Chapter 5 further addresses an observed experiential phenomenon that, if this path is followed, recoveries from other significant but unrelated physical and mental health difficulties may also occur: "There are those, too, who suffer from grave emotional and mental disorders, but many of them do recover if they have the capacity to be honest" (Anonymous, 2001, p. 58).

Based on their experiences, accomplished through *action*, the early members of Alcoholics Anonymous concluded that through

75

honestly utilizing the suggested steps for recovery, including the adoption of a spiritual philosophy toward life, they have experienced significant positive changes in their lives. The following quotation is has been affectionately labeled, "The Promises:"

> "If we are painstaking about this phase of our development, we will be amazed before we are half way through. We are going to know a new freedom and a new happiness. We will not regret the past nor wish to shut the door on it. We will comprehend the word serenity and we will know peace. No matter how far down the scale we have gone, we will see how our experience can benefit others. That feeling of uselessness and self-pity will disappear. We will lose interest in selfish things and gain interest in our fellows. Self-seeking will slip away. Our whole attitude and outlook upon life will change. Fear of people and of economic insecurity will leave us. We will intuitively know how to handle situations which used to baffle us. We will suddenly realize that God is doing for us what we could not do for ourselves." (Anonymous, 2001, pp. 83-84).

Thus, for a client who presents with an addictive disorder, we see that the greatest probability for therapeutic success is through a spiritually based remedy. In review, the spiritual process begins with the therapist guiding the client to contemplate 'God's' question: "Where are you?" When the client gains a general sense of where he or she stands in relation to his or her 'God,' then the client needs to begin the process of coming to terms with, and gaining a basic understanding of, who 'God' is to them. As clients begin to find the 'God' of their own conception, they begin the delicate process of trusting and relying on this 'God,' and eventually surrendering to the *Spirit* who they have come to believe can rescue them from their debilitating addictions. [*This process may be helped by reviewing Steps 1-4 with the client. (Anonymous, 2001, p. 59).*]

Once clients have gained contact with the 'God' of their own understanding and have come to realize their *location* in relation to their 'God,' then the counselor can assist clients in listening for 'God's' invitation to "*Come.*" Answering 'God's' "*call*" requires action on the part of clients. That action will cause them to turn towards 'God' and begin taking 'steps' that will eventually lead them closer to this 'God' "of their own conception." As clients come into closer proximity to 'God,' they will gain a greater understanding of 'His' principles and nature. "When we drew near to Him, He disclosed Himself to us!" (Anonymous, 2001, p. 57) (Jones, 2006) [*This process may be assisted by reviewing Steps 5-9 with the client. (Anonymous, 2001, p. 59).*]

Once initial abstinence is achieved, then intensive therapeutic work may be necessary to "get down to causes and conditions." However, cessation from addictive practices is a *one-day-at-a-time* process and is *never* to be taken for granted. The client will require daily maintenance of his or her "spiritual condition." (Anonymous, 2001, p. 85). Thus sobriety, through this daily maintenance of spiritual connectedness, will be continually necessary for sustained recovery. [*The process of continued daily maintenance will be greatly assisted by reviewing Steps 10-12 with the client. (Anonymous, 2001, pp. 59-60).*]

With Sobriety,
All Else
Is Possible

Chapter 10

Counselor Considerations in Spiritually Based Addictions Counseling

Source of Healing Power

Spiritually based counseling can have significantly catastrophic pitfalls. One such pitfall is the counselor's own attitude and relationship with spiritual principles. Whether or not they possess a spiritual or religious basis, most counselors enter the profession in order to be of service to others and provide helping therapy to those in need. Thus, if done with care and love, good counselors are able to guide their clients in spiritual directions. Initially, the therapeutic power of all counselors is derived from the client's perception that the counselor possesses the therapeutic power in the healing process. Christian and spiritually based counselors channel actual power by opening themselves to the will of the Spirit and allowing 'God' to use them as a conduit of His healing resources. This is accomplished by merely reducing counselor ego and allowing 'God' to *steer* the process. Conversely, in Addictions Therapy, the counselor who interjects unyielding self-will and egoism into the therapeutic process does not have the client's best interest in mind. Thus, the client's successful treatment may be non-existent or short lived.

Despite their own spiritual proclivities, clinicians can successfully facilitate clients to integrate their own spiritual or religious principles into the recovery process. Successful addictions therapists assist the client in understanding that the therapist is there to facilitate the *Client - Spirit* relationship and that the healing *power* necessary to assist in combating the client's addiction will come from the *Spirit,* or 'God,' of the *client's* own conception. Questioning with regard to the client's spiritual inclinations and preferences will assist the therapist with values clarification and selection of supportive ideologies. It is recommended that the client's spiritual growth be included into the treatment or recovery plan. (Harvard Medical School, 10-2007) (Corey, 2007).

Counselor Qualifications

Traditionally, even the most successful, revered, and seasoned psychologists and therapists have experienced difficulty in reaching those clients with alcoholism and other addictive disorders. In the chapter titled "There is a Solution," the book "Alcoholics Anonymous" discusses this phenomenon thusly:

"Highly competent psychiatrists who have dealt with us have found it sometimes impossible to persuade an alcoholic to discuss his situation without reserve." "But the ex-problem drinker who has found this solution, who is properly armed with facts about himself, can generally win the entire confidence of another alcoholic in a few hours. Until such an understanding is reached, little or nothing can be accomplished.

That the man who is making the approach has had the same difficulty, that he obviously knows what he is talking about, that his whole deportment shouts at the new prospect that he is a man with a real answer, that he has no attitude of Holier Than Thou, nothing whatever except the sincere desire to be helpful; that there are no fees to pay, no axes to grind, no people to please, no lectures to be endured - these are the conditions we have found most effective. After such an approach many take up their beds and walk again" (Anonymous, 2001, pp. 18-19).

As such, subsequent to its beginnings in 1935, Alcoholics Anonymous developed practices and procedures for mutual support groups, one-on-one assistance, fellowship gatherings, and selfless methods of reaching out to prospective members. A.A. was growing because it offered a proven solution to alcoholism. Since the publication in 1939 of the book "Alcoholics Anonymous," where this movement's 12 Step spiritual program was laid out, the practices of Alcoholics Anonymous have been examined by prominent mental health professionals in an attempt to understand why and how this new program has proven successful whereas their secular-scientific medical model had rarely achieved more than short-term success.

Of course, upon examination, the obvious initial reason for the apparent success of the Alcoholics Anonymous program was that of: "One alcoholic talking to another alcoholic." Laying aside the spiritual aspect of the program, the conclusion drawn by professional examiners was that counselors of those with alcoholism and other addictive disorders could and should be recovered from an addiction as well. Thus early on, a prerequisite for becoming an alcohol, drug, and/or other, addictions counselor was to be sober, or successfully recovered, for a specified period of time, and be personally involved a recovery program as well. Beginning in the mid 1970's, in the absence of any medical or psychiatric addiction counselor education programs, private organizations for the training of Alcohol and Drug Counselors began to emerge. Using experiential knowledge, they developed formal competency criteria, counselor training programs, and certification procedures, but only recently have States began to require that treatment facilities hire counselors who have been certified by an approved training agency. (Breining, et al., 2008).

Most other licensed mental health professionals were deemed 'qualified' to provide therapy to addicted individuals. However, the majority of these clinicians had received little, if any, formal training to do so. Currently, since training and certification of addictions counselors is now mandated, and additional training in the field of addictions is compulsory for those seeking licensure as therapists and counselors in the many other mental health related areas, the previous prerequisite for addiction counselors to be in 'recovery' themselves is no longer viewed as applicable or necessary.

Consequently, those individuals wishing to become addictions counselors need only fulfill the education and training requirements for certification as a drug and alcohol counselor. Previous experience shows that these new counselors, who have not personally experienced the sting of addictions, or the struggles necessary to overcome them, may be at a distinct disadvantage for achieving meaningful success in the addictions recovery field. However, having a disadvantage does not mean that they cannot become exceptionally successful counselors. It does suggest that they should nevertheless become acutely aware of this issue and develop specific skills to help them better relate to and assist their clients.

Complex Problems - Simple Solutions

Secular-scientific mental health professionals have difficulty successfully treating alcoholics, and those with other addictive disorders, because they are only trained and equipped to treat a portion of the client's problems. Alcoholism, as were many other addictive disorders, was initially described as a disease that is *three-*

fold in nature. It was defined as: 1) An allergy of the body; 2) An obsession of the mind; and 3) A spiritual malady. (Anonymous, 2001, pp. xvi. xxvi, 23, 64). Secular-scientific counselors are typically only equipped to treat the client's mental obsession and possibly to touch on the allergic reaction aspect of alcoholism. As such, the spiritual aspect is largely left untreated.

Part of the continuing success of the lay-professional, non-scientific approach to recovery from alcoholism is that those with alcoholism are being assisted by those who have personally recovered from alcoholism. They offer an *observable* solution. That solution is typically the spiritual 12 Step program that originated in Alcoholics Anonymous. (Anonymous, 2001, pp. 92, 58-60). The new client is thus being provided with guidance by a counselor who has taken the same steps and followed the same spiritual path that they are offering to the client. Additionally, what is remarkable about the spiritual approach is that *the solution* it contains covers a significantly wide array of presenting mental and physical conditions and ailments. By comparison, in the secular-scientific approach, the first step in treatment is to *define the problem*. A recent article exploring medicinal drug treatments for alcoholism stated of *the problem* of alcoholism:

"The complexity of alcohol's effects on the body and brain creates further difficulties. Alcohol influences almost every neurotransmitter system in the brain and has a specific affinity for none. It may also cause long-term changes in neuronal gene expression (activation). Different types of alcoholism - early-onset and late-onset, severe and mild, with and without a family history - may be different genetically and respond differently to drugs and psychosocial treatments. It is unlikely that any single approach will ever work for all alcoholics. These complications make the potential availability of more drug treatments especially welcome."

"Finding a reliable treatment for alcoholism has been a frustrating quest... all common psychosocial treatments have been found equally and moderately effective. So physicians have turned to drugs. So far the results are inconclusive and some still hesitate to treat any substance abuse problem with a drug." (Harvard Medical School, 7-2005, pp. 5, 3)

In contrast, the spiritually based approach to treatment *does not* emphasize or focus on *the problem*. The focus of Addictions Therapy is on *the solution.* Complex problems have simple solutions. "When the spiritual malady is overcome, we straighten out mentally and physically." (Anonymous, 2001, p. 64). When *the solution* is practiced daily, *the problem* goes into remission and significantly diminishes. The body and mind appear to rapidly self-rejuvenate with the cessation of alcohol use. Similar benefits are obtained as a result of secession of other substances and addictions.

Roadblocks to Successful Counseling

Counselors and therapists, who have not personally experienced addictions, and subsequent recovery, are initially at a disadvantage for treating those with alcoholism and other addictive disorders. However, recent trends indicate that they are capable of overcoming these initial rapport-building disadvantages and becoming successful in the field of Addictions Counseling. Still, there are some roadblocks to success that should be overcome before ethically working with those clients seeking recovery from alcoholism and other addictive disorders. Some of these roadblocks are noted here:

- *Personal use of alcohol and/or licit or illicit drugs:*

    Prospective counselors and therapists should examine themselves for dependency. If not dependent, it may be useful to cut back significantly or stop drinking and/or using altogether. Regardless, counselors should be clean and sober when working with clients.

- *Personal religious or spiritual beliefs, or lack thereof, may interfere with the spiritual identification and growth of the client:*

    Avoid interjecting personal beliefs into the client's self-assessment process.

- *Counselors who have not experienced addiction and recovery may have difficulty relating to the feelings and emotions of those with addictions:*

    Such therapists must understand the disease aspect of these disorders and not view their clients as weak willed, morally deficient, purposefully deceitful, or remiss in rule following. New therapists should seek advice from more seasoned counselors and ask alcoholics and addicts to describe how they 'feel' internally. Consider and compile these descriptions of emotion for future reference, display empathy and understanding to the client, but be unwavering on *the solutions* aspect. Above all, be honest with the client as to personal experiences or lack thereof.

- *Personal difficulties with, or susceptibility to, co-dependency issues:*

    A thorough understanding of the codependency issue is essential to the counseling process and critical to the client's recovery. (O'Neal, 2011)

- *Ego, Client:*

    Ego in the client is one of the most significant roadblocks to the attainment of a spiritual recovery. Ego is also a block to other therapeutic interventions as well. Clients often enter counseling with a humble willingness to try. However, as they begin to regain a sense of normalcy, ego returns, and as is the course with addictions, clients may begin to feel that there is *nothing wrong* with them. Thus, their cooperation in the counseling process may become less than wholehearted. (A.A. members often state that they suffer from a disease that tells them they don't have a disease).

- *Ego, Counselor:*

    The client will detect undue ego in any counselor, but will do so very rapidly in therapists who are not in recovery themselves. Client detected unwarranted ego in the counselor will significantly reduce any chance the client has of recovery - with that particular counselor. It should be understood that in spiritually based therapy, neither the client nor the counselor are the source of *Power*. Recovery is spiritually centered and directed. Recognition of the spiritual 'center' in therapy helps to reduce ego and promote humility in both client and therapist.

Therapeutic Goal: Sustained Recovery

Thus, the field of therapy and counseling of alcoholics and others with addictive disorders is open to all helping professionals who have a willingness and desire to enter this broad arena. The medical profession is also included in this definition as they routinely interact with addicted clients and attempt to utilize medications and other medical treatments to assist clients with recovery. Alcoholics

Anonymous itself claims no monopoly on the treatment of, or the recovery from alcoholism. Nor, in the spiritual realm, does A.A. specify a singular approach to 'God.' It merely offers a solution that has proven effective and worked for those of its members who have displayed enough desire, willingness, and honesty, to earnestly try. (Anonymous, 2001, pp. xxi, 95).

Of course, since the spiritual approach has proven its effectiveness in the treatment of addictions, techniques for assisting counselors in bringing clients into the healing realm of the *Spirit* is the central focus of this book. And, assisting clients to achieve lasting recovery is the goal of the spiritual approach in Addictions Counseling. Other approaches may be effective with some clients. However, to date, no other approach has achieved a higher or longer lasting rate of success than the spiritual approach.

The spiritual approach appears to assist the client in achieving abstinence in a shorter period of time, helps the client reconcile with life more rapidly, and is instrumental in the achievement of sustained abstinence and long-term recovery. As such, it is postulated that, until a more effective and reliable method of treatment is available, the spiritually based counseling approach should be the central focus for Addictions Therapy.

Notwithstanding that which has been discussed thus far, it should be noted that Addictions Counseling, by whatever approach, is necessarily short-term. However, *addictions are forever*. Therefore, regardless of the approach used, the success or relapse of the client will be based on his or her ongoing participation in recovery and continual therapeutic involvement. Counselors should review all available continuing care programs and guide their client towards participation in such care. Regardless, it must be emphasized and re-emphasized that continuing care is vital to sustained sobriety and that it is the *sole responsibility of the client.*

Prolonged recovery will often be predicated on the foundation laid in initial treatment. Spiritually based 12 Step programs have proven exceedingly beneficial in providing such readily available and continuing aftercare, as well as providing initial foundational spiritual concepts. In the early stages of sobriety, counselors may be rightly concerned about some of their client's conceptions of 'God,' and of the ideologies into which clients place value. However, it should be realized that, with abstinence, spiritual growth will commence. Once spiritual growth begins, it will evolve as the *Spirit* starts the process of reshaping client's lives. As such, the client's conception of 'God' and his or her ideological values will evolve as well. A client's early membership in spiritually based 12 Step programs will assist the clinician in facilitating this personal spiritual acquisition process. Helping professionals will serve their clients well in guiding them toward active participation in such programs.

With Sobriety,
All Else
Is Possible

Chapter 11

Attributes of an Effective Addictions Counselor

Sources of Therapeutic Power

Counselor attributes used here are drawn from all therapeutic approaches. So far, this study has not compared the Biblical-Christian based counseling approach to the spiritual approach in that they have much in common. The spiritual approach also retains much commonality with the secular-scientific approach with regard to general techniques, etc. As discussed previously, the distinction between these three approaches with regard to counselor attributes is their source of *Power*.

In the *secular-scientific approach*, counselors typically feel that therapeutic power rests within *themselves* by virtue of their training, experience, degrees, licensing, etc. Likewise, clients may feel that therapists, by virtue of their qualifications, possess the power to solve their problems. Thus, the client projects perceived power into the counselor. However, if the client detects an incompetency in the clinician, power projection evaporates and counseling is ineffective.

Religious or Christian counselors may or may not have similar backgrounds in education, training, experience, etc., as the secular-scientific therapist. Nevertheless, they may hold additional titles such as priest, deacon, minister, rabbi, elder, etc. They may also possess other religious qualifications and/or training that provides them with great insight into the realm of the Spirit. However, these religious clinicians believe that the source of healing *power* in their counseling does not come from themselves as counselors, but rather from external sources such as the God of their religious denomination, Christ, the Bible, etc.

In the *spiritual approach*, the therapeutic power is derived from the client's own understanding and/or conception of a '*God*' that is personal to them. With this base of therapeutic *power* in mind, the attributes listed here will utilize an eclectic vantage point for consideration and review. If available, the *spiritual presence* within the counselor contributes as well to the overall *spiritual presence* in the counseling setting. It becomes an additional source of power available to the developing *spiritual presence* within the client. In such situations, both client and counselor become receptive to integrating with the *spiritual presence* that possesses the healing power contained in this spiritual approach to recovery. Even in its *silence*, the *Power* of this *Presence* is palpable.

The attributes of an effective Addictions Counselor follow:

General Counselor Attributes

- *Honest, forthright:*
  The client must view the counselor as a person of spiritual integrity. Any hint at dishonesty, rule bending, lapses of ethics, undue familiarity with the client, etc. will lead the client to believe that the rules need not be followed. This will lead the client to believe that the counselor does not have full faith in the therapeutic process, nor is he or she fully committed to it. Consequently, the likelihood of a successful therapeutic outcome is nil.

- *Empathetic:*

  The client must perceive that although the counselor adamantly believes in the therapeutic process and treatment plan, the therapist also understands the plight and pain of the client's situation. The counselor must be available to listen to the client's hopes, fears, ideas for growth, and dreams for the future. The counselor must project an undertone of compassion and understanding for the client, yet remain firm in directing the client to take the required actions regardless of his or her emotional state. (Clients with addictive disorders are not bad people trying to get good, they are sick people trying to get well.)

- *Confident:*

  The counselor must present an aura of confidence; Confidence not only in him or herself and the therapeutic process, but in the *Spiritual Power* that is capable of producing miracles. "The central fact of our lives today is the absolute certainty that our Creator has entered into our hearts and lives in a way which is indeed miraculous. He has commenced to accomplish those things for us which we could never do by ourselves." (Anonymous, 2001, p. 25)

- *Model, Prepare, Organize:*

  The counselor must be prepared to meet with the client and be well organized. The therapist must *model* the attributes that he or she is attempting to instill in the client: be on time, appropriately attired, well groomed, have materials on hand, have reviewed notes of previous sessions, is ready to pursue new therapeutic territory, and be spiritually well grounded.

- *Non-judgmental:*

    Clients should feel free to safely express their innermost thoughts and deeds without fear of disapproval or condemnation. The client may feel some aspects of their story are reprehensible. As such, they will test the counselor's reactions with smaller bits of information. If the counselor exhibits a judgmental attitude to the smaller pieces of information, the client will not share further of themselves with this counselor, and possibly with any future counselor. The internal spiritual readiness of the counselor will be evaluated by the client in this manner.

- *Be Present:*

    The client should feel that the counselor is emotionally and spiritually present and available to the client - in both time and space. The clinician needs to be attentive, not distracted (phone and electronic devices off), and the counselor's outside issues set aside prior to the start of the session.

- *Knowledgeable:*

    The counselor must be knowledgeable of all aspects of Addictions Counseling and the recovery process. Addictions counseling differs from other forms of counseling in significant ways. Counselors must be aware of these differences to be able to assist the client in spiritual recovery efforts. Such will represent a shift in philosophy for therapists who also counsel in areas other than addictions.

- *Truth Seeker:*

    Counselors, who honestly desire to present the best possible therapy to their clients, are themselves seekers of truth. *Truth* is essentially the goal of all counseling. Flawed research and/or emotionally based decisions often produce conclusions that, when acted on, are not always in the best interest of the client. With regard to this topic, during one of his talks, then Pope Benedict XVI stated: *"Departure from [truth]... or silence about it, in an effort to provide pastoral care, is neither caring, nor pastoral. Only what is true can ultimately be pastoral."* (Benedict XVI, 2011). Counselors should continually update their skills and training. They should also research and study issues on their own to ensure they are providing their clients with accurate and truthful information. They should practice too, the same openness to spiritual guidance that they suggest to their clients.

- *Openness to Spiritual Movement:*

     Regardless of the approach used by the counselor, the client may feel an emotional upheaval that will necessitate an alteration of the treatment plan and/or the direction the counselor had predetermined for the client. Accommodations in such plans need to be made to facilitate the client's access to his or her spiritual contact. In other words, the therapist must be open to changing the treatment plan as indicated by *spiritual movement* within the client.

- *Obtain Religious Information:*

     Counselors may wish to contact Clergy members of various faith communities. Tell them of the counseling role played in the spiritual growth of people in recovery. Ask them to explain their faith in terms that could be used in a way that would be beneficial to clients. Such clergy may be good referral sources should the therapist have clients who are of, or have questions about, a particular faith.

- *Spiritually Attuned:*
  Counselors need to be in tune with themselves and with the values they feel are most precious and righteous. This attribute is common among counselors who have experienced addiction and recovery. When this attribute is present in the counselor, the counselor is perceived by the client to be in harmony with self, others, and their surroundings. This perception gives a sense of comfort to the client and invites them to join in harmony with the therapist and the recovery process.

Attributes of a Biblical Counselor

The attributes of a Biblical based Counselor are delineated in the Bible and are presented here for informational purposes. (NAB, 1992 Isaiah 11:2-3). The attributes a Biblical Counselor shall possess are:

- *"The Spirit of the Lord shall rest upon him:"*
  The counselor shall have the presence of God in him/her and be guided by His presence.

- *"A Spirit of wisdom and understanding:"*
  The counselor will have the discernment to assist with the making of prudent decisions and be empathetic towards the spiritual needs of the client.

- *"A Spirit of counsel and of strength:"*
  The counselor will have the ability to appropriately advise, guide, and direct the client, and will be forthright

with resolve for instilling in the client what is just, righteous, and prudent for actions.

- *"A Spirit of Knowledge and of fear of the Lord:"*
  The counselor will be learned in the ways of righteousness, and in appropriate procedures, and in the doings of things. The counselor will have great respect for, and be accountable to, the Lord.

- *"And his delight shall be the fear of the Lord:"*
  In the sense presented here, the term "fear of the Lord" means to stand in awe, to hold in great respect and esteem, to revere, to hold oneself accountable to, to recognize and appreciate the magnitude of this Supreme Authority. The therapist recognizes that God possesses the *power* in the counseling process and acknowledges that it is God's healing *power* and authority at work, not that of the counselor. The counselor delights in being a transformational tool of the Lord.

Attributes of, and Techniques for, Spiritually Based Addictions Counselors

In helping to facilitate the connection of spirituality into a client's recovery program, the counselor may wish to utilize some of the 'tools' listed here. As mentioned previously, it is not necessary for the therapist to be 'in recovery,' nor to have a spiritual connection to their own conception of a Power Greater than Themselves, i.e., 'God.' However, it is necessary that the clinician adhere to basic spiritual, or moral, principles.

Aside from a basic desire to assist others, counselors typically enter the helping professions with an eye towards self-exploration and self-understanding. If they have not done so, counselors who are entering the field of Addictions Therapy, may wish to explore concepts of their own spiritual nature. Regardless of the outcome, their doing so should aid them in assisting their clients, and in understanding themselves more fully.

In his discussion of the Christian faith the former leader of the Roman Catholic Church noted that: "Faith, by its very nature, must give rise to theology, [and] must question itself on the reasonableness of faith." (Benedict XVI, 2011). In other words, *faith* has always encouraged the study of *itself* with *reason,* and to reject that which is discovered to be untrue. Theology is the study of *faith*. True theology studies *faith* with *reason* in search of, and in comparison to, *truth*. To date, *reason* has only proven to draw truth seekers closer to *faith*, but the answers they've discovered are their own. So, as *faith* explores *itself* with *reason*, it would be advantageous for those within the addictions recovery field to continually explore their own conception of, and connection to, a '*Power* Greater than themselves.'

The therapist's role in 'treatment' will, by its nature, be short lived. Therefore, a spiritually self-aware counselor may be able to assist clients to a greater understanding of their own spirituality more rapidly and effectively than a counselor who is not. Although it is not required that the counselor have a personal spiritual connection, it is recommended. Regardless, the clinician needs to know that the client's gaining of a spiritual connection is vital and will greatly assist in sustained recovery. The counselor should be aware too that the client's maintenance of a spiritual connection will significantly improve the chances of avoiding relapse. Therefore, at a minimum, the counselor should possess the tools to assist in guiding the client toward a connection to a *Spiritual Power Greater than Themselves.*

Following are some suggested concepts counselors may use to assist clients in gaining a spiritual connection and facilitating spiritual progress:

- *Client Spiritual self-evaluation:*

   Assist clients in the exploration of their own previous experiences with religion. Childhood feelings toward their own conception of 'God,' or their lack thereof, should be explored. Assist the client in describing their *ideal* 'God.'

- *Guide the client in the learning of Spiritual Principles:*

   Guide the client in learning of the spiritual aspects of 12 Step programs. The initial and basic concepts of 12 Step programs were derived from the Oxford groups and consisted of: "moral inventory, confession of personality defects, restitution to those harmed, helpfulness to others, and the necessity of belief in and dependence upon God." (Anonymous, 2001, p. xvi). Clients are often very averse to talk of religious and spiritual matters. They should be assured that they are merely learning about an aspect of recovery methodology that has been helpful to others. Once they learn of the spiritual aspect, as presented in 12 Step programs, ask them to compare the *spirituality* of these recovery programs to their own current and previous conceptions of 'God.'

- *Group discussion:*

   Use group discussions to solicit the views and experiences of other clients with regard to their spiritual conceptions. Often, hearing of the spiritual experiences of others in recovery assists the client in the consideration of seeking a personal spiritual connection. The personal testimony of others is sometimes more influential than the subtle guidance of the counselor.

- *Spiritual acceptance is not immediately necessary:*
  Regardless of whether or not a client initially accepts the spiritual aspect of recovery, instill in them that their acceptance of spiritual concepts is not necessary. What is necessary is a 'willingness to believe' that there is a '*Power* greater than themselves.' Seeking spiritual assistance has been beneficial to others, but if clients choose not to avail themselves of it, it is not necessary at present. Clients should continue on their journey of personal recovery. Spirituality comes in many forms. Often clients discover their own spiritual connections elsewhere in their recovery process. Regardless, active participation in counseling and aftercare is imperative. Therefore, clients must reach deep within themselves for the *power* to do what is required to achieve lasting freedom from their addiction. Once this is tried, clients often see the value in accepting spiritual assistance. They seek such assistance when they realize that the solution to their addiction problem may be beyond the power of their human will. They may also come to the realization that 'God' has been present with them and caring for them all along.

[Within 12 Step groups, when a newer member is having difficulty with the spiritual concept or with 'finding God,' it is often suggested that they pick anything to use as a "Higher Power." Some have used a Doorknob; a Tree; The Group; etc. It has also been suggested by older members that if the newer member is having difficulty finding or believing in

'God,' that they can borrow the older member's Higher Power until the newer member can find one of their own: "If you believe that I believe, and you think I'm doing okay, then borrow my God, until you find your own." In talking about 'God' with a reluctant new client, it is often helpful to use acronyms to describe 'God,' like: God = Group of drunks; God = Good ol' dude; God = Good orderly direction; Take the word 'Good' and spell it with one 'o;' etc.]

- *"Fake it till you make it:"*

    This is a time honored phrase heard in 12 Step programs which can be used with regard to acceptance of spiritual principles. It implies that the client doesn't have to understand '*it*,' doesn't have to like '*it*,' doesn't have to want '*it*,' but just has to *do* '*it*.' "Bring the body and the mind will follow," is another related conceptual phrase.

    [This A.A. principle was also studied for its application to treatment of another addictive substance. Cognitive Behavioral Therapists discovered the truth and effectiveness of this "fake it 'til you make it" *Behavioral* principle while studying cocaine addicts. They discovered, what A.A. has known, that the effect of the *Cognitive* aspect of 'Cognitive Behavioral Therapy' (CBT) was limited in its treatment with addicts. *Talk* therapy and cognitive *reasoning* with addicts, with the intent of appealing to their intellect to convince them that it would be in their own best interest to stop using cocaine, has proven time and again to fail in achieving its goal. However, the researchers did discover that the 'B' *Behavior* aspect of CBT appeared to work well when applied first before the 'C' *Cognitive* aspect (Hence: BCT). This aspect of "fake it till you make it" is to instruct the client to take the actions (Behavior) suggested: follow the principles of a Higher Power (even if it's not yours), keep coming back ("Let's ignore how you 'feel' right now, we realize you may not want to be here, but just stay today, and then come back tomorrow"). Eventually 'the mind' (Cognition) will catch up with the body – and 'the mind' will be amazed at the progress the body achieved while 'the mind' was 'away.']

This concept indicates too that addictions are not purely a result of distorted thinking, but rather a whole body disease. Active participation of clients in their own recovery process, particularly in a (spiritual) 12 Step program has been proven to be a vital aspect in lasting sobriety. (Harvard Medical School, 5-2008) (Weiss, et al., 1996). As such, *regardless* of the client's current thoughts or feelings, taking the suggested *action* of participating in A.A., other spiritually based 12 Step recovery programs, or another type of aftercare, brings about changes in behavior that eventually leads the client to positive mental changes, and spiritual and emotional growth.

- *Prayer and meditation:*
  Counselors should encourage clients to explore prayer and meditation. This is consistent with Step 11 to improve conscious contact with the 'God' of the client's understanding. If the client asks, a good prayer to suggest would be the 3rd Step prayer found on page 63 of the book "Alcoholics Anonymous" (Anonymous, 2001). However, it is better to ask the client to suggest some prayers. If prayer is not acceptable to the client, then the therapist may wish to suggest meditation techniques that provide for relaxation, reflection, and quiet introspection. Such techniques might include mindfulness meditation, yoga, personal quiet time,

etc. No matter the prayer or meditative method, instill in the client that this is a time to open oneself to the intuitive thought process; a time to be receptive to one's heart; a time for listening to the Creative Power of the Universe. Regardless of the prayer or method, honest prayer negates ego and opens the heart and mind to a source of power *outside* of one's self. *Prayer changes those who pray.*

- *Free-will. Why do we have it?*

  The client, when discussing the possibility of opening him or herself to 'God' might ask: "If God gave me free-will, what is its purpose?" "How would He want me to use it?" A possible response might be that: "God may desire that people should use their will, to willingly seek and do His will." That people possess free-will, indicates that 'God' did not create humankind to be obedient, mindless robots. People can think and do anything they choose. Consider that 'God' created us in the hope that people would freely choose Him. 'God' granted the power to choose. As such, the client is free to continue to indulge in their addiction, if that is what they choose to do. However, remind the client that currently, at this point in their recovery process (today), they have chosen not to do so. Such a choice, abstinence, would likely be 'God's' will for them as well. The book "Alcoholics Anonymous" discusses this topic thusly: "Every day is a day when we must carry the vision of God's will into all of our activities. "How can I best serve Thee - Thy will (not mine) be done." These are thoughts which must go with us constantly. *We can exercise our will power along this line all we wish. It is the proper use of the will.*" (*emphasis* added) (Anonymous, 2001, p. 85).

- *Spiritual Beings; Faith:*

   "We are not human beings going through a temporary spiritual experience. We are spiritual beings going through a temporary human experience." "Faith is not about everything turning out ok; Faith is about being ok no matter how things turn out." (Unknown). Counselors may wish to utilize specific thought provoking inspirational phrases, sayings, and quotes such as these to stimulate the client's transcendent spiritual thoughts and discussions. Such contemplative phrases assist in internalizing and personalizing 'God's' *presence* in the client's life.

- *Ego reduction and the acquisition of Humility:*

   One of the primary factors that help the client eventually gain spiritual insight is learning to get-out-of-self (ego) by being of service to others and/or putting the concerns of others above those of self (humility). Such service to others is beneficial only if done without expectation of return. The counselor may assist the client in achieving this worthy goal by assigning service related tasks. Clients will feel the *presence* of the *Spirit* when they realize the opportunities and blessings of being capable of providing true service to others. In this realization, they will begin to understand that they are but 'fellow travelers' in life, no better and no less deserving than their fellows. That they have a right to be here, as do others, that their service to others does not make them less than, but helps them understand that when they are concerned about others, they are not thinking about themselves. True self-esteem or esteem for self (not ego), is obtained by performing acts that are estimable.

- *Basic living skills:*

Spiritual connectivity often comes from learning basic living skills. Alcoholics and those with other addictive disorders have often lost the ability to perform basic living skills. The importance of retrieval and performance of these basic skills is often ignored as irrelevant by clients, and their counselors as well, but are vital to continued sobriety. Counselors may need to assist the client in establishing (re-establishing) a daily routine, a schedule of events, and a 'Things-to-Do' list. Such routines and events might include: establish a bed time that ensures time for adequate sleep. Tasks may include: wake up on time, make the bed, shower, eat breakfast, brush teeth, set a regular time for prayer and meditation, eat appropriate meals at regularly scheduled intervals, get to work on or before starting time, give the employer a full day's work (and a bit more), don't lie, cheat, or steal, come home after work, share chores and family responsibilities, establish a regular schedule of recovery meetings, make time to be present to family, seek regular medical and dental attention, take care of household tasks such as washing dishes regularly, laundry, trash, yard care, etc. The client may resist such tasks, and the therapist may feel that the client doesn't or shouldn't need to be instructed in these basics. However, the establishment of structure and routine facilitates recovery and brings a sense of stability to lives that didn't realize they were chaotic and out of control. Self-regulation and self-discipline are often foreign concepts to those with addictions. Additionally, a build-up of undone chores and unfulfilled responsibilities produces excess stress and anxiety. This emotional tension can in turn lead to a return to use of addictive substances and/or behaviors for their ability to *instantly* deliver emotional relief.

- *Slogans:*

    Counselors should not discount the power of the simple slogans that have evolved in recovery programs. The power of these slogans is sometimes masked by their simplicity. Yet, these slogans are capable of preventing relapse in times of need. The *spirituality of simplicity* in the slogans is sometimes recognized when clients have used them to help withstand a crisis. In gratitude of that *power,* clients have looked toward the heavens and whispered: "Thank you." Some contend that 'slogans' are the *handrails* of recovery, because they are there to 'hold-on to' in times of need. As such, these handrails will prevent the client from 'slipping' and falling. Counselors may wish to task clients to compile a list of slogans they've heard in 12 Step meetings and describe the meaning of each. Some of these slogans may include:

    - God = Good ol' Dude
    - God = Group of Drunks
    - God = Good Orderly Direction
    - God = 'Good' spelled with one 'o'
    - Can't find God? Borrow mine until you can find your own
    - We have a wrench for every nut
    - If you pray, why worry? – If you worry, why pray?
    - Stop living in the problem – Start living in the solution
    - One day at a time
    - Easy does it (but do it)
    - First things first
    - So what, do it anyway
    - Think, Think, Think (Think it through to the end)
    - Think before; afterward is too late
    - 1 is too many; 1,000 isn't enough

- Suit up and show up
- Expect a Miracle
- Relax, God is in charge
- Keep on the firing line of life
- Misery is optional
- What's your motive? – Is it any of your business?
- Don't take yourself so darn seriously
- KISS = Keep it Simple Sweetie
- Surrender to Win
- Complex problems have simple solutions
- Let go and let God
- We were born to be Happy, Joyous, and Free
- We absolutely insist on enjoying life
- This too shall pass
- Adopt an attitude of gratitude
- Progress not perfection
- More will be revealed
- Resentment is the #1 offender
- Fake it till you make it
- Don't like what you're getting?-Stop what you're doing
- Act as if
- (c) That God could and would if He were sought
- Faith without works is dead
- You don't get run over by the caboose (1st drink hits you)
- The more you know - the more you know you don't know
- It's about the journey, not the destination
- *Addiction* is turned *to* - when you turn *away* from *God*
- I'm just the Worker Bee, God is management
- Sobriety: going Up the Down escalator – must keep moving
- You're only as sick as your secrets
- Expectations are premeditated Resentments
- Don't leave 5 minutes before the miracle

- H.A.L.T. = Don't get too: Hungry, Angry, Lonely, or Tired
- The set of the Sails, not the wind, controls your direction
- Etc.. (Anonymous, 2001) (NAB, 1992) & (Unknown).

- *Dual diagnosis:*

   Many clients will have a dual diagnosis. As such, they may be prescribed medications. Research has shown that those people who take psychiatric medications are less likely to recover through A.A. or other 12 Step programs (Harvard Medical School, 7-2007). Consequently, adaptation to a spiritual approach of recovery may be inhibited as well. Such individuals often feel that they already possess a (chemical) solution to their problems. They may feel they are plagued by difficulties that only another chemical will remedy. Therefore, clients who take such medications may not possess the *urgency* for recovery typically seen in those seeking immediate help in alleviating the pain produced by their addiction. Prescribed medications may tend to prevent clients from "hitting bottom" and thus the motivation to take immediate *action* for recovery is often not present.

   However, regardless of whether the client is prescribed medications or not, the clinician should still provide the client with spiritual supports and tools as they may nevertheless prove effective, if not now, then possibly sometime in the future. Counselors should be aware that dually diagnosed individuals may not display the same recovery growth rate as other clients. This is not to say that clients on mood altering medications won't also benefit from a spiritual solution. However, based on the type of medication and related therapy, if any, these clients are typically not fully open to consideration of the spiritual aspect of recovery nor are they usually willing to fully participate in a 12 Step recovery program.

Willingness is the *key* to successful recovery. Prescription medications often rob the client of willingness to participate, not only in sobriety programs, but in everyday life events as well. Regardless, these prescribed medications, if taken strictly as prescribed by their physician, may be critical to the client's emotional and/or physical wellbeing and thus are not to be discouraged. However, within ethical guidelines, the counselor may wish to discuss the client's condition with the prescribing practitioner and alterations in medication type and dosage may be made with concurrence and monitoring.

- *The Role of the Counselor is to: "Disturb the Comfortable and Comfort the Disturbed"* (Finley Peter Dunne):

   Pain is often the touchstone of growth. More often than not, people do not grow if they are *comfortable*. It is from pain that they seek remedy and relief. It is in this *seeking* that the client *grows* spiritually. It is in the *pain* of 'hitting bottom' and subsequent 'surrender' that emotional walls are taken down and masks are removed; self-centeredness is diminished; and '*who you are*' is revealed. 'God' responds to the alcoholic prayer: "God help me," and begins to direct the client's thinking and actions. *When* clients begin working their way out of painful situations, *then* counselors can effectively offer *comfort,* empathy, and encouragement.

- *Invite 'God' into the process:*

   Probably the most important aspect of spirituality based Addictions Counseling is the *invitation*. There is no definitive process of doing this. Inviting 'God' into the counseling process not only acknowledges the *presence* of His healing power, but also instills a sense of accountability, and a more honest interaction. This displays then that the *Power* is *not* within the counselor. The counselor merely facilitates the process. The client's progress in recovery is then between the client and the 'God' of the client's own conception. For those with addictions, the concept of inviting 'God' into the recovery process becomes a necessary *daily* occurrence.

- *Determine the client's "Location":*

    As previously discussed, the counselor asks the question of clients: "Where are you?" (Jones, 2006). The counselor invites clients to discuss their own conception of 'God' and then discuss *where they are* in relation to the 'God' of their own conception. Once this *location* is determined, then the therapist should guide the discussion in an attempt to ascertain the steps necessary for the client to come into closer contact with their conception of 'God.' Counselor and client should determine what actions are necessary for the client to live life in a manner that will produce greater harmony with 'God.' As clients live their lives in a fashion more pleasing to their 'God;' as clients become more 'attuned' to, or in sync with, this 'God,' feelings of tension and anxiety diminish. As decisions and actions continue in harmony with the client's perception of 'God's' will, life's difficulties will begin to diminish as well. Such harmony is an indication that the client's *location* is moving closer to their 'God.'

"Restlessness, irritability, and discontentment" are words used to describe those in the grip of addictions whose *location* is becoming more distant from their 'God.' These are the feelings addicted individuals usually experience just prior to relapsing. These disconcerting feelings are described as those that are instantly relieved with the resumption of, or relapse into their addiction. The emotional disharmony associated with restlessness, irritability, and discontentment may eventually be more satisfactorily overcome through the use of spiritual principles as a replacement for addictive practices. (Anonymous, 2001, p. xxvi).

- *Have you heard "God's" Call?*

    Inquire if the client has heard "God's" "*Call.*" (Jones, 2006). If the client has not perceived *'God's' invitation*, the counselor might wish to discuss: That, just as 'God' has been invited to participate in the recovery process, 'God' invites the client to *come* into spiritual contact with Him. 'God' invites the client to move toward Him; to move into His mercy and love; to follow in His ways; and commence His way of living. Invite clients to *listen* with a *still*, open heart, and open mind. Remind the client that this *calling* is by their own conception of 'God,' a conception that 'God' Himself likely instilled in order to facilitate this *spiritual* relationship. Remind the client that he or she is truly *worthy* of 'God's' care, and *invitation* to *come*.

With Sobriety,
All Else
Is Possible

Chapter 12

Indicators of Spiritually Based Recovery

Is Sobriety Enough?

What are the fruits of this spiritual recovery process? How does one determine if a spiritual transformation, or spiritual recovery, has taken place in the client? How does one measure success? The first answer that comes to mind is: "Cessation of addictive behaviors." Surprisingly however, this is not always the best measure of success. Of course sobriety, or the cessation of an addictive behavior, is the overall goal. Nevertheless, experience shows that anyone can *stop* an addictive behavior. It's the *staying stopped* that presents the most difficulty. Longevity in sobriety is therefore the actual true measure of successful recovery.

Individuals with long-term recovery have noted from experience that those who are afflicted with addictive disorders tended to stop maturing and growing emotionally once they learned that they could use a mood-altering substance or behavior instead of dealing with a problem or emotion. As such, cessation of drinking, using, etc., often leaves the client with few, if any, coping skills for handling life's everyday problems - no matter how seemingly insignificant. One individual, who had been sober several years, shared an account of his own current *reaction* to one of life's events: "If my neighbor goes out in the morning and his car doesn't start, he calls the Auto

Club. If I go out and my car doesn't start, I call Suicide Prevention. My plans are ruined, my day is a disaster, I'm a failure, even my car hates me, and my life is over. I've done everything asked of me, and now my car won't start! My initial reactions are drinking or suicide."

This statement illustrates the dilemma typically faced by those in recovery. Where were his *tools* for living? Life's minor frustrations may often seem like major life-altering catastrophes. Although very irrational to the outside observer, such insignificant events may produce significant over-reactions that can often lead to a return to drinking, using, or other addictive behaviors; or they can also lead to other devastating reactions such as suicide [The permanent solution to a temporary problem]. As such, a key aspect of the recovery process involves assisting the client in the acquisition of the *coping skills* necessary to appropriately handle life's events – good and bad, regardless of their severity. Belief in; reliance upon; and accountability to; a Power greater than one's self, will greatly assist in preventing such events from turning ruinous.

Recovery is a lifelong endeavor. Despite learning the coping skills necessary to handle life's events, those skills tend to fade over time and must be relearned and/or reinforced frequently. The man who said he felt suicidal when his car didn't start related that even after all his years in recovery he still doesn't have the rationality to control his *initial reactive impulses*. He went on to say that even though anger and/or depression are often his initial impulses, he now has the *spiritual tools* to overcome these emotions and knows he no longer has to act on his impulses. He stated that now, instead of allowing himself to become upset, he stops and reflects on the situation, asks for spiritual guidance, evaluates the importance of the situation, sets priorities, and takes the required action to remedy the problem. For the typical 'normal' person, this process is 'intuitive'

112

and occurs subconsciously within a few moments. For a person in recovery this must be a well-reasoned, step-by-step process.

For those with an addictive disorder, this process requires conscious implementation of a 'learned' response which initially instructs the individual to: "Stop! – Do not react! - Wait until the situation is rationally evaluated and an appropriate reaction/response is formulated!" Within the time it takes for contemplation of this learned response, the threat of irrationally over-reacting has usually passed. The next learned step is to 'be still' and ask 'God' to provide an idea for a proper course of action. Seemingly miraculously, within a few moments, an intuitive thought occurs that provides answers to appropriately solve the situation at hand. (Anonymous, 2001, pp. 84, 86).

Feelings of Disharmony in Sobriety

Initially, many people with addictive disorders haven't learned how to live and function appropriately within their normal day-to-day environment. Further, they typically: *don't know*, that they *don't know*, how to live and function appropriately. But they do know that *something* is amiss and that they don't feel comfortable 'in their own skin.' They feel out-of-sync with their current situation and don't understand why. "What's wrong with *them*?" or "Is it *me*?" are typical questions they ask themselves. In addition to feeling at odds with society, whether true or not, people with addictions often feel that they are unworthy, inadequate, unwanted, and unloved. Such feelings tend to exacerbate the client's disharmony with the world around them, and thus magnify the disharmony within themselves. Alcoholics describe these feelings as being: *"restless, irritable, and discontented."* (Anonymous, 2001, p. xxviii).

These are *the feelings* that are *masked* by addictions and are the ones most often responsible for relapse. With abstinence, these are *the feelings* that return with a vengeance and whose intervention and remediation have eluded counselors and therapists worldwide for the past millennia. So far, the restoration of internal *harmony* has only been achieved through the intervention of a "Higher Power;" Thus, a *spiritual solution.* This solution is otherwise described as a *spiritual experience.* The *awareness* of the *Presence* of 'God' in one's life tends to bring with it internal (spiritual) harmony. It is defined in Appendix II of the book Alcoholics Anonymous as follows:

> "With few exceptions our members find they have tapped an unsuspected inner resource which they presently identify with their own conception of a Power greater than themselves. Most of us think this awareness of a Power greater than ourselves is the essence of spiritual experience. Our more religious members call it "God-consciousness."" (Anonymous, 2001, pp. 567-568).

Understanding and Internalizing 'God's' Love, and Signs of Recovery

As discussed earlier, regarding their very *existence*, newer clients often ask: "Who am I?" and "Why am I here?" The answer may seem obscure at first, but the response is truly simple: *Who are they?* They *are*: "Children of God" and they are *here* because 'God' seeks their willing companionship, friendship, and love. People with addictions often do not comprehend 'God's' love of them. A Biblical example of 'God's' personal love and acceptance is found in Luke chapter 15:1-7 (NAB, 1992), in the "Parable of the Lost Sheep." In this parable's analogy, the Shepherd (God) leaves his flock (all other people) and goes out in search of his "lost sheep" (those who feel unworthy of Him). He rejoices when He finds the one who is lost.

114

"...There will be more joy in heaven over one sinner who repents than over ninety-nine righteous people who have no need of repentance." "Rejoice with me for I have found my lost sheep."

Having the *knowledge* of 'God's' care and love hastens the client to take the Third Step. In step 3 the client makes a decision to: "Turn our will and our lives over to the care of God, *as we understood Him.*" (Anonymous, 2001, pp. 59, 63). Once this decision is made, and the 3rd step prayer said, clients entrust their lives to 'God's' care. Based on knowledge of 'God's' love for them, an understanding of *life's meaning* begins to appear. At this point, a feeling of calm and comfort often overcomes the client. With this occurrence, some of the following signs, or fruits, of *spiritual* recovery begin to appear:

- They display a sense of inner peace, comfort, and possess a general sense of calm
- "People of faith have a logical idea of what life is all about"
- "...Spiritually-minded persons of all races, colors, and creeds [are] demonstrating a degree of stability, happiness and usefulness..."
- They seem to "rise above their problems"
- They possess a sincere concern for others
- They display reduced selfishness, self-centeredness, self-seeking, and self-pity
- Spiritually oriented people are less interested in 'self' and more interested in contributing to life and their community
- They are able to successfully face life's challenges large and small
- They begin to lose formerly debilitating fears
- They begin to repair personal and business relationships
- Financial difficulties begin to be resolved

- With proper motives, people who exhibit spiritual fitness can go anywhere normal people may go without fear of relapse
- Ego diminishes, but confidence and self-esteem improves
- They commence to build or rebuild their lives and become self-supporting, productive members of society
- They seem to possess the tools necessary to overcome issues in life which used to be puzzling to them
- They seem to have gained a desire to learn and to become more physically, mentally, and spiritually fit
- They tend to grow emotionally with great rapidity
- They appear to become healthier and less prone to mental and medical disorders and disease

Those who have accepted a spiritual connection often begin to make positive changes in their thoughts, behaviors, and reactions to life. Ironically, clients are usually unaware that these changes are occurring. Others can see positive changes in the client long before he or she is aware of them. They observe that the client has undergone a "personality change" sufficient enough "to bring about recovery…" Then, after recognizing that changes have occurred in themselves, clients realize that they have "undergone a profound alteration in their reaction to life," that this change could not have been achieved without spiritual assistance, and that this personality change, and other changes, "could seldom have been accomplished by years of self-discipline". (Anonymous, 2001, pp. 49, 55, 62-63, 84, 100-101, 567-568).

Even though these lifestyle changes usually take place over a period of a few months, counselors and significant other people in their lives are often astounded at the magnitude of the client's change in feeling and outlook. Such results can sometimes be seen in those who recover on a *non-spiritual, self-will* basis as well. Termed

116

"white knuckled sobriety," their results do not appear to be as deep rooted nor as lasting as those who recover on a *spiritual* basis. Such client's too, though 'sober' often lack the serenity and peaceful altered attitude that comes with a conscious *spiritual* connectedness.

Of course *time* is a significant gage of the effectiveness of recovery through a spiritual remedy. Sustained cessation of addictive behavior is an indicator that the client's own conception of 'God' is at work in his or her life. When clients appear to be practicing spiritual principles, seem to have a sense of peace and serenity in their lives, and have enjoyed a period of sustained sobriety, the lives of these clients may appear to have new meaning:

- They have assumed personal responsibility for their own lives and actions
- They are grateful for their opportunities in life
- Their motives in and for personal interactions are typically pure
- They are trustworthy
- They keep their word and fulfill their obligations
- They are of service to others
- They possess a sense of inner fulfillment
- They avoid unnecessary conflict

If these qualities can be observed in the client, the counselor who has utilized the spiritual approach can take a certain satisfaction in knowing that their assistance and interventions were beneficial and helpful. Counselors will know that these interventions were designed to lead their client to the source of *Power* that could solve their client's personal maladies. In knowing the client's background, and observing the magnitude of growth within such a brief period of time, the clinician begins to comprehend that the client was in fact, *beyond human aid.* The counselor realizes that a spiritual intervention did for the client what the client was unable to do for him or herself, and that this *spiritual power* was instrumental in the client's rapid and miraculous transformation.

The Workings of the Spiritual Approach

The spiritual approach to Addictions Counseling produces recovery not by specific religious rituals nor by analysis into the deep recesses of the client's psyche, but that is not to say that these practices may not be of assistance. The spiritual approach inspires recovery by introducing the client to the 'God' of his or her own conception and facilitating the client's relationship with that spiritual entity. Remarkably, when the client gains conscious contact with his or her Creator, addiction begins to lose its grip. Of course, the 12 Steps are part of this process. Step 12 emphatically states that a "spiritual awakening" will have occurred, at some point during this process, as "the result of [taking] these steps."

As stated, this "spiritual awakening" of clients with their *Creator,* may occur at any time in the process - but of course, the growth process will need to continue. Continuance of the process will serve to strengthen the spiritual bond. This spiritual bond brings the client into closer harmony with 'God.' As in tuning a musical instrument, an out-of-tune note will produce wavering 'beats' of dis-harmony. With the process of bringing the *off* note into tune (taking the Steps), the 'beats' of dis-harmony diminish and the notes blend into the harmonious synchronicity of a single tone. The two begin to move as *one.* In religious terms, this process of reconciliation, or bringing a dis-harmonious note into tune, may also be referred to as the process of atonement. Of interest, if the word 'atonement' is broken up into its parts, we get the words 'at-one-ment,' which of course implies that the results of the process of *atonement* is to become *at one* with 'God.' When *at one* with 'God' the client *experiences* His *Presence.* This phenomenon is noted in the book "Alcoholics Anonymous" as: "...*Awareness* of a Power Greater than ourselves is the *essence* of *spiritual experience*" (Anonymous, 2001, p. 568)(*emphasis* added).

As the client becomes *attuned* to 'God,' his or her whole outlook on life is miraculously changed. This *change* may occur in many different forms, some subtle, some dramatic. But the *change* is indicative that *faith*, the key ingredient necessary for a successful recovery, has been accepted and ingrained into the psyche of the client. Even if a client cannot yet accept the concept of a spiritual solution, if they are able to *act-as-if* 'God' exists in their life, they will begin to display signs of behavioral change. Such signs may include: a reduction of ego, an increase in humility, a willingness to participate in life more cheerfully, etc., and they will begin to sense a feeling of greater fulfillment and joy in life - and the 'tuning' process with 'God' begins. Some relevant statements from the book "Alcoholics Anonymous" related to this process follow:

- "If a mere code of morals or a better philosophy of life were sufficient to overcome alcoholism, many of us would have recovered long ago. But we found that such codes and philosophies did not save us, no matter how much we tried. We could wish to be moral, we could wish to be philosophically comforted, in fact, we could will these things with all our might, but the needed power wasn't there. Our human resources, as marshaled by the will, were not sufficient; they failed utterly. Lack of power, that was our dilemma. We had to find a power by which we could live, and it had to be a Power greater than ourselves."

- "… A spiritual liberation from this world, people who rose above their problems. They said God made these things possible…. Actually… deep down in every man, woman, and child, is the fundamental idea of God. It may be obscured by calamity, by pomp, by worship of other things, but in some form or other it is there. For faith in a Power greater than ourselves, and miraculous demonstrations of that power in human lives, are facts as old as man himself."

- "We finally saw that faith in some kind of God was a part of our make-up…. Sometimes we had to search fearlessly, but He was there. He was as much a fact as we were. We found the Great Reality deep down within us. In the last analysis it is only there that He may be found."

- "But just underneath there is deadly earnestness. Faith has to work twenty-four hours a day in and through us, or we perish. Most of us feel we need look no further for Utopia. We have it with us right here and now."

- "Then they outlined the spiritual answer and program of action which a hundred of them had followed successfully. Though I had been only a nominal churchman, their proposals were not, intellectually, hard to swallow. But the program of action, though entirely sensible, was pretty drastic. It meant I would have to throw several lifelong conceptions out of the window. That was not easy. But the moment I made up my mind to go through with the process, I had the curious feeling that my alcoholic condition was relieved, as in fact it proved to be."

- "... Receiving strength, inspiration, and direction from Him who has all knowledge and power. If we have carefully followed directions [the Steps], we have begun to sense the flow of His Spirit into us. To some extent we have become God-conscious. We have begun to develop this vital sixth sense."

- "Quite as important was the discovery that spiritual principles would solve all my problems. I have since been brought into a way of living infinitely more satisfying and, I hope, more useful than the life I lived before. My old manner of life was by no means a bad one, but I would not exchange its best moments for the worst I have now. I would not go back to it even if I could."

(Anonymous, 2001, pp. 44-45, 55, 16, 85, 42-43).

The Counselor's Therapeutic Ability is Based on Client Perception

To the addictions counselor, creating an atmosphere conducive to facilitating a spiritual connection between the client and his or her 'God' may appear to be a daunting task. It is as non-specific and yet individualized as the clients are themselves. As in preparing for all other methods of therapy, much knowledge and preparation is required of the counselor. Yet, all preparation and knowledge is not sufficient to ensure a successful outcome. *A counselor's ability to set the stage for meaningful therapeutic progress is contingent on the client's perception of the counselor's abilities and on the counselor's and client's openness to spiritual intervention.* After all, the restorative *Power,* that is the 'active ingredient' in this therapeutic approach, is *Spiritual.*

121

Early in the counseling career of this writer, fear of not possessing sufficient knowledge and skill to appropriately benefit clients brought the realization that a certificate on the wall does not a counselor make. In questioning this author's own therapeutic abilities, the advice of a trusted Spiritual Advisor was sought. After carefully listening, the advisor smiled knowingly, and in comforting tones he stated: "You have prepared well and you have much knowledge and skill. Your clients will assume you have the requisite knowledge. However, that knowledge is only useful to a point. Remember that they *won't* care how much you know - but they *will* always know how much you care." The advisor's implication was that, with the client's best interest foremost in mind, and with a *spiritual* star to steer by, a positive therapeutic process will ensue. The counselor only needs to trust in his or her training and skill, and be willing and open enough to receive and integrate intuitive spiritual guidance. In so doing, gentle direction and appropriate assistance will be provided. For the newer counselor, enter the process, and leave the results up to the 'God.' Allow the client's conception of 'God' to guide the process - then watch as miraculous transformations and events occur. "Expect a miracle."

With Sobriety,
All Else
Is Possible

"There are only two ways to live your life. One is as though nothing is a miracle. The other is as though everything is a miracle."
— Albert Einstein

Chapter 13

Is Prayer Beneficial?

As discussed previously, prayer and meditation are cited as essential elements of the spiritual recovery process. In order to further develop the concept of Spirituality in Addictions Counseling, available research into the power of prayer is explored. In meetings of Alcoholics Anonymous and in those of other 12 Step programs, an opening prayer is sometimes utilized. And, in virtually all of these groups, a closing prayer is traditional and recited by all members who wish to do so. During the closing prayer, group members stand in a circle and hold hands. Someone is asked to lead the group in the closing prayer. The prayer is usually selected by the member who has been asked to lead the closing prayer. However, since the inception of Alcoholics Anonymous, "The Lord's Prayer" has been the traditional prayer of choice. Neither a 'format' for the conduct of meetings, nor a prescribed prayer, is delineated in the book "Alcoholics Anonymous." These practices were in place before the book was written. These loose 'rituals' or 'traditions' have been handed down since the A.A. program's foundation.

Within the book "Alcoholics Anonymous," prayer is suggested for use in specific times and settings. The eleventh step, which is one of the three steps (10, 11, and 12) that are designed for daily use, states: "Sought through prayer and meditation to improve our conscious contact with God *as we understood Him,* praying only for knowledge of His will for us and the power to carry that out." The A.A. book also suggests morning and evening prayer and meditation. Additionally, it notes various specific instances where the reader is encouraged to pray and "ask God" for such things as: instruction, strength, an intuitive thought, etc. Similarly, the reader is coached in how to pray and/or what to pray for, such as: "We usually conclude the period of meditation with a prayer that we be shown all through the day what our next step is to be, that we be given whatever we need to take care of such problems. We ask especially for freedom from self-will, and are careful to make no request for ourselves only. We may ask for ourselves, however, if others will be helped. We are careful never to pray for our own selfish ends." The book "Alcoholics Anonymous" discusses the topic of prayer with experiential confidence with statements such as: "It works, if we have the proper attitude and work at it." (Anonymous, 2001, pp. 59, 84-87).

It should be noted that *intercessory* prayer is not a prescribed aspect of 12 Step programs. Intercessory prayers are prayers that are prayed singularly or in a group specifically asking 'God' to intercede for someone other than themselves. Although such prayer is frequently done, such as offering a moment of silence for those who still suffer, it is not a tenet of 12 Step programs to pray for self or others within the context of regular meetings. However, it has been the experience of some members that intercessory prayers, prayed for those against whom resentments are held, can be very freeing. Specifically, one of the personal stories presented in the A.A. book is often referenced by members regarding the topic of intercessory prayer. It is titled "Freedom Form Bondage." (Anonymous, 2001, pp. 544-552). It describes praying for the "health, prosperity and happiness" of those against whom a resentment is held. The experience of the writer was that if this process is persisted in, the feelings of "bitterness, resentment and hatred" will be replaced with "compassionate understanding and love." Thus, the person who is praying this intercessory prayer is released from the bondage of resentment. It may be inferred that: *Prayer changes those who pray.*

Prayer, as described in the book "Alcoholics Anonymous," is based on the experiential results obtained by the participants, and subsequent participants who have availed themselves of A.A. and/or other 12 Step programs. As such, for informational and discussion purposes, a review of the scientific literature of studies designed to measure the effectiveness of prayer was undertaken. Although the results of prayer are evident to the participants, the effectiveness of prayer has not been necessarily proven through currently available scientifically based research.

Research on the Effectiveness of Prayer

Intercessory prayer: Praying for the needs and wellbeing of others. A 1999 review of then existing studies on prayer indicated that intercessory and individual (self) prayer provided a more positive outcome in every study reviewed. The reviewed literature on *intercessory prayer* included: a double-blind study of patients in a coronary care unit; group prayer and the laying on of hands over individuals who did not have access to medical care; the effect of prayer on the germination of plant seeds; and prayer's effect on the growth of micro-organisms in petri dishes. Each of these studies displayed "significant" results in comparison to their control groups. This cited research project also asked for the opinion of a prominent atheist regarding the positive results of these studies concerning the effectiveness of prayer. He responded that he felt the positive results noted were not due to prayer, but to the *placebo* effect of prayer. He indicated that the sense of comfort and peace brought about by prayer, faith, religious involvement, and connectedness to a community of caring people, instead of God's response to prayer, were the salient factors responsible for producing the results. However, he could not explain why plants germinated more rapidly and fungi grew more or less rapidly based on the application of prayer. (Williams, 1999).

Individual prayer: 'Individual' prayer is self-prayer. The individual prays for self and others. Self-prayer is a reaching out to 'God' in an attempt to gain greater contact and connectedness. Studies of *individual prayer* appeared to produce results similar to those noted in the studies of *intercessory prayer*. These studies also controlled for and included individual involvement in religious organizations and personal Bible reading. The studies reviewed included: a study that investigated the effects of prayer on lowering blood pressure; a study of twins which indicated that those who prayed and were more spiritual were less prone to smoking and alcohol related problems. In other research, a study of the feeling and outlook of severely debilitated hospitalized patients indicated that those who enjoy a spiritual connection are in better spirits and have a better prognosis than those who did not seek such a connection. These studies of individualized prayer were also reported to have very positive results in relation to their controls.

The most extensive studies of the effectiveness of prayer, and other interventions, MANTRA and MANTRA II (Monitoring and Actualisation of Noetic Trainings) were conducted on acute coronary patients through Duke University and other participating medical institutions. These studies did not report such positive findings. These studies researched the effectiveness of outside therapeutic measures termed "Noetic." Noetic means 'mind based' or 'non-pharmacologic.' These therapies included music, imagery, and touch

(MIT); and prayer. The MIT (Music, Imagery, and Touch) interventions included: soothing music, guided imagery, and touch therapy. The *intercessory* prayer interventions included: local and distant prayer; varied and numerous religions and denominations; patients who knew that they were being prayed for; and patients who did not know. The religious faith, if any, and strength of the patient's spirituality were also considered. These noetic interventions were compared against *standard therapies*. These studies were termed the MANTRA feasibility pilot (Krucoff M. W., et al., 2001) and MANTRA II studies (Krucoff M. W., et al., 2005).

Although not significant in its findings, MANTRA's pilot study tended to imply that prayer originating from off-site showed a positive influence in patient outcome. However, any outcomes observed were not statistically outside the realm of chance. A more extensive follow-on study, MANTRA II, found similar minimal improvements, but the results again did not meet the statistical criteria for clinical significance. A statement from the second study indicated: "In MANTRA II, we studied two noetic strategies in patients undergoing coronary revascularization: an unmasked bedside combination of music, imagery, and touch, and a double-masked, off-site array of combined congregational prayers. Neither therapy alone or combined showed any measurable treatment effect on the primary composite endpoint of major adverse cardiovascular events at the index hospital, readmission, and 6-month death or readmission."

According to the researchers, some of the problems in conducting the studies, and in interpreting their findings for the sections concerned with prayer were: time of onset, duration, type, type of client knowledge, intensity, number of participant prayers, faith of the participant prayers, etc. In other words, "what *dosage* should be used for which type of patient?" Although the MANTRA studies were as well choreographed as possible, they only tended to bring to light the vast number of variables which need to be accounted for and controlled in order to gather accurate data from which meaningful conclusions could be drawn. Nevertheless, the researchers appeared to be looking for data from which they could assess the prayer needs of the client and prescribe a specific *dosage* of prayer in order to assist with the client's recovery.

Interestingly, in a follow-up article regarding the MANTRA studies, some of the study's contributors discussed their observations. Although not statistically relevant, nor specifically measured in the studies, the researchers indicate that a primary factor noted in a number of the studied cases that showed positive outcomes, was the *personal spirituality* or *individual faith* of the patient. They noted that one patient, who had been prayed for from 'off-site,' recovered well. His results were attributed to the 'off-site' prayer. However, the researchers speculated that these positive results could have been credited to the patient's *personal faith* rather than to the off-site prayer regimen. Was it the offsite prayer, or the patient's faith that produced the positive results? The researcher, Susanne Crater, Ph.D., stated "Did those distant well-wishers help [this patient] during his angioplasty? Or did his own faith (The patient had commented to researchers that: "While I'm not a church-going man, I believe in the Lord") help pull him through? Can the prayers that soothe Spirits also heal bodies?"

Another MANTRA researcher, Harold Koenig, MD, speculates that since "MRI brain scans have documented the deep state of rest, calm, and relaxation that envelopes the brain of a person who is meditating. Since prayer can resemble meditation, the effects of the two processes may be similar." That researcher stated too that "persons who depend on religious beliefs to cope enjoy better survival rates following heart surgery than those who do not." He noted that "religion provides "a world view," a perspective on problems that helps people better cope with life's ups and downs. Having that world view helps people integrate difficult life changes and relieves the stress that goes along with them. A world view also gives people a sense of meaning and purpose in their lives." Dr. Koenig further indicated that "people who are more religious tend to become depressed less often. And when they do become depressed, they recover more quickly. Because depression has been linked to negative outcomes in heart disease and other conditions, that has consequences for their physical health and the quality of their lives. The role of religious faith in healing is so important that," Koenig believes, "physicians should obtain spiritual histories as part of their medical and social histories. Such a history could be used to find out how patients cope with illness, the sort of support systems available to them, and any strongly held beliefs that might influence medical care."

Dr. Koenig observed that "Prayer is a person's primary link to the Creator. Whether there is a Creator or not, people believe there is. And if you believe in God, sometimes God responds by doing miracles -- by breaking into the natural order of the universe in a way scientists and doctors cannot understand. It doesn't happen all the time. But it does happen often enough to give many of us the desire to learn more about how to harness this mysterious force to enhance the healing process. And it gives patients, and the people who love them hope." (Duke University Medicine, 2006).

Following release of the findings from MANTRA II, the BBC headlined articles titled "'No health benefit' from prayer" (BBC News, 2003) and "Prayer 'no aid to heart patients'" (BBC News,

2005). These BBC reports did not speculate on the individual *faith* of the study patients, but did comment that the music, image, and touch therapy (MIT) did appear to assist by reducing patient stress. However, the MANTRA II did not list the stress reducing effects of MIT as a finding of the study. The BBC did invite views on the study from theologians and other experts who are quoted as stating: "Even if you believe in the power of intercessory prayer, such a trial is doomed to failure because it "puts God to the test" - and there are clear instructions in the Bible not to do this." The Bishop of Durham, the Rt Rev Tom Wright, said: "Prayer is not a penny in the slot machine. You can't just put in a coin and get out a chocolate bar." "This is like setting an exam for God to see if God will pass it or not." Dr. Richard Sloan, from the New York Presbyterian Hospital, described the concept of a prayer "dose," as "absurd." He said: "It requires us to abandon our understanding of the physical universe."

The New York Times (New York Times, 2006) also quoted Dr. Sloan. They reported him as stating "The problem with studying religion scientifically is that you do violence to the phenomenon by reducing it to basic elements that can be quantified, and that makes for bad science and bad religion." This same New York Times article also noted a 1997 University of New Mexico study on intercessory prayers. That study involved 40 alcoholics in a rehabilitation facility. It found that the participants who knew they were being prayed for actually experienced worse outcomes. Such an adverse outcome could then be viewed as a lack of faith or a purposeful disrespect for the faith of those praying for them. Such disrespect, on the part of those being prayed for, could surely thwart any positive prayer based results. Nevertheless, Bob Barth, Spiritual Director of the prayer group "Silent Unity," and other individuals involved in healing prayer, view such studies as "interesting," but speculate that prayer research is in its infancy with much further study ahead. As Mr. Barth stated "We've been praying a long time and we've seen prayer work, we know it works, and the research on prayer and spirituality is just getting started."

Other studies of prayer have found more positive results. Some of these studies include:

- *"Does God answer prayer? ASU research says 'yes'"* (Physorg.com, 2007).

   David R. Hodge, who conducted an analysis of 17 major studies on the effects of intercessory prayer, stated of the studies that regard prayer as ineffective: "...This research suggests otherwise. This study enables us to look at the big picture. When the effects of prayer are averaged across all 17 studies, controlling for differences in sample sizes, a net positive effect for the prayer group is produced. This is the most thorough and all-inclusive study of its kind on this controversial subject that I am aware of," said Hodge. "It suggests that more research on the topic may be warranted, and that praying for people with psychological or medical problems may help them recover." As such, he indicated that prayer, although not suitable for use as the primary method of treatment, should be used in a supplemental role as "meta-analysis indicates that prayer is effective."

- *Prayer Relieves Mind in Many Ways, Study Finds* (Bryner, 2010).

   "Getting on your knees and looking to the heavens may really bring comfort during tough times, new research finds." This study suggests that people pray "in order to manage hard situations, including illness," and find relief from "emotions such as sadness and anger." It also notes that "most Americans believe that God is involved in their everyday lives and concerned with their personal well-being." The results of this study "showed that in general that God or another figure from religion acted as a support system for the participants. This figure had certain perceived characteristics such as being loving, powerful, and caring, that influenced why participants sought him or her out. But unlike a flesh-and-blood shoulder to cry on or an abusive partner to rail at, God was available whenever and wherever the participant reached out. If they vented their anger to that abusive partner, the result was likely to be more violence, but they could be angry at God while praying, without fear of reprisal." This report suggested too that, with these positive results in mind, "mental health professionals should consider prayer as an *interaction* instead of a one-sided act," and that they "can try to develop similar, non-prayer ways to accomplish these tasks." In other words, Therapists can try to substitute the positive implications of prayer onto a "therapy program that will be sure to include positive, self-esteem-boosting feedback that can counteract negative feedback in patient's lives."

- *Study: Prayer Turns Aside Anger* (Heagney, 2011).
  This study is not necessarily of intercessory prayer, but rather exhibits the effectiveness of prayer for the individuals who pray. "Researchers have found that people who pray when they are angry feel less angry, behave less aggressively and are less likely to think that others are out to get them." This Ohio State University study "was conducted using three separate experiments on students. The results showed that prayer had the power to quell anger in all three." Some salient comments included: "It didn't matter whether the

praying subjects were religious or went to church, prayer helped pretty much everybody;" "When you pray you're spending that period of time cultivating a sense of altruism, which makes you happy anyway;" "Prayer works because people often ask God for forgiveness, as we look for God's forgiveness in our lives, it will prompt us to be more forgiving of other people;" Secular research indicates that "religiosity and prayer are good for physical and mental health." Of the research Rev. Greg Tidwell stated: "I do believe God is at work in our lives, but I do not believe that divine grace can be empirically measured by research. By the very nature of faith, it's beyond what researchers are going to be able to document."

- *"Prayer Research: What are We Measuring?"* (O'Mathuna, 1999)

  In a 1999 research review on the effectiveness of intercessory prayer, several studies were evaluated and discussed. It was found that certain aspects of some of the studies show a strong correlation between intercessory prayer and positive clinical outcomes in some measured categories, but not all. It also discussed various studies in which more positive results were seen in the control group, who received no intercessory prayer. What is important in this study is its appropriate in-depth analysis of the variables surrounding prayer, the individual being prayed for, those who are praying, the nature of illness, the approach to and type of prayer, the scientific method for measuring and interpreting results, and God's will. O'Mathuna's study concludes that God answers prayer, but not in any consistent pattern or prevalence. The study also concludes that for some individuals, healing is not always God's will. The individual's will and God's will are not always aligned. Some believe that from the perspective of eternity, God "takes" people, for their own good, at a point in their lives when they are "closest" to Him. Or, he may "heal" them when He has need of their future service to Him or to others. He may need them to be in-place to "touch" someone in the future. As such, God's will for people is always the unknown variable in research on prayer. Science treats God's *will* as it does God's *laws* or, as the laws of nature. Science believes that God's will is, or should be a constant, and thus a predictable 'if - then' ingredient in any study. Obviously, this is not the case, thus complicating any scientific study on the effectiveness of prayer.

- *Spiritual Connectedness vs. Religious Activity* (Waldron-Perrine, Rapport, Hanks, Lumley, Meachen, & Hubbarth, 2011)

    A Wayne State University study, although not specifically addressing the topic of prayer, studied the topic of religion and spirituality in rehabilitation outcomes for patients who suffered with the consequences of traumatic brain injury. This thorough study examined potential healing assistance of existential social support, participation in religious activities, and what the study termed "religious well-being" which was defined as the patient's individual spirituality or "a sense of connection to a higher power." The study related that the positive effects of both existential social support and participation in religious activities were well documented. These factors are known to produce a certain level of therapeutic assistance. As expected, those positive effects were also noted in the Wayne State study. However, the study concluded that those patients who indicated a faith in, a personal relationship with, and/or feelings of connectedness with their own "Higher Power" exhibited significantly better emotional and physical rehabilitation outcomes. The study states: "The findings of this project indicate that *specific facets of religious and spiritual belief systems do play direct and unique roles in predicting rehabilitation outcomes whereas religious activity does not.* Notably, *a self-reported individual connection to a higher power was an extremely robust predictor of both subjective and objective outcome.*"

Research Summary of Prayer

On the level of personal prayer, being in conscious contact with one's Creator tends to bring on a state of calm, comfort, and inner peace. In all cases of prayer, the spiritual intent and results are based on *confidence in* the power of 'God,' and *not* in the power of scientific research. One way to ensure that prayer is ineffective is to pray in a clinical scientifically prescribed ritualized format *without* 'faith.' (Yet, 'God' may answer anyway). One might have 'faith' in science, but science itself does not answer prayers. As in proving that man would never fly, science cannot predict what 'God,' and man's 'faith,' can do. Just as in man's flight however, science can explain how some material activities were accomplished, but it cannot make them so, nor can it detract from them.

Where, when, why, and how prayer works, or doesn't work (or doesn't *appear* to have worked), is for science yet to prove. Nevertheless, all attempts to disprove the miraculous have failed. Probably more so than in churches, the miracles of prayer and the intercessions of 'God' are observed and reported in Alcoholics Anonymous and in other 12 Step recovery programs derived from it.

If this fact were not so, A.A. and other such programs would no longer be in existence. The prayers offered in these programs are often those that some religious bodies and scientific researchers claim would not work. The prayers in these 12 Step programs are simple, prescribed, ritualistic, and repetitive. However, they are humble, obedient, service oriented, and usually filled with faith and gratitude. From the desperate initial Alcoholic's prayer of "God help me," to the daily prayers of "How can I best serve Thee Lord, Your will, not mine be done." Such prayers are often followed by asking 'God' to reveal His will for them and to give them the power to be of service to Him and to others, and to carry out His will. Science, and some religious institutions, might *prescribe* that an alcoholic pray for *sobriety*, but as discussed elsewhere, drunkenness, or other addictive disorders, were only a symptom. Hence the 'alcoholic's prayer' *is not*: "God, get me sober." The alcoholic's prayer *is*: "God, help me."

'God's' will is not known, so the success or failure of prayer is not readily scientifically quantifiable. What is known, however, is that whether one believes in 'God' or not, *prayer changes those who pray*. A saying often heard in 12 Step programs is: "Expect a Miracle;" which is, in-and-of itself, a profession of 'faith.'

Placebo and Nocebo Effects

In light of speculation by some researchers that the general success of the spiritual approach to Addictions Therapy, and the effectiveness prayer, may be primarily due to the placebo and/or nocebo effect, available research of those effects was examined. The results are presented here for consideration and review. Although, in certain instances, the effects produced by placebos and nocebos are remarkable, they have not proven to be effective in combating addictions. They have not proven to be the source of *Power* attributed to 'God' and prayer, as many have suggested. If placebos wielded such power, they would themselves be extremely addictive.

In 1955 Dr. Henry K. Beecher, a Harvard Medical School Doctor, wrote of his wartime observations and subsequent study findings that described the placebo effect. (Beecher, 1955) He described this effect as a phenomenon whereby a patient's *perception* of pain was altered or alleviated by the use of a dummy pill or placebo. He speculated that this effect may be produced by the power of suggestion or the perception that the pill patients received contained a remedy, and their minds had imagined that their pain was gone. Subsequently, numerous studies have been conducted that dispute the findings of Dr. Beecher, and appear to have done so in many instances. However, the phenomenon remains, and is an evident and measurable force in nearly every scientific study where inert medications or treatments are used in control groups.

The opposite of the placebo effect is the nocebo effect. In Latin, the term *placebo* means "I will please" and *nocebo* means "I will harm." The nocebo effect is typically the result of negative 'conditioning.' This negative conditioning will characteristically solicit a negative response from the conditioned individual under certain circumstances. A recent article on this topic noted examples of the nocebo effect as people who "faint at the sight of a needle," or "start to sweat as soon as they walk into a dentist's office," or people who "get nauseated or even vomit on entering a room where they recently received chemotherapy." An additional nocebo effect is that of suggestion. Such suggestive power may increase pain or discomfort. Such suggestions may come through comments such as "be prepared, this may hurt;" or "It might be better if you look the other way;" etc. (Harvard Medical School, 5-2011).

It is the power of the *nocebo effect* that is the prime mover in 'aversion therapy.' Aversion therapy has been tried extensively on those with addictive disorders in an attempt to cure them of their addictive obsessions. Such therapy usually produces early positive results. However, without reinforcement, such results fade over time as the strength of the addictive disorder overcomes the aversion's nocebo effect. Additionally, consider that addictions produce their own severe negative consequences that *are* sufficient enough to 'avert' most people. Nonetheless, to those with alcoholism and/or other addictive disorders, such 'aversive' consequences are not sufficient to deter continuation of addictive behaviors.

Placebo, Addiction, and Spirituality - Power Source Comparison

With regard to the nature of the healing effect of *Spirituality* in Addictions Counseling, one might speculate that the *Power* of the *Spirit* was nothing more than an effect similar to the placebo reaction; that the *Power* of the *Spirit* was nothing more than suggestive – as is that of the placebo. (Williams, 1999). Although it may be true that the *aversion* therapy utilized in some non-spiritual recovery programs may produce results based on the *nocebo* effect, those results for true alcoholics and other addicts are typically short-lived. Such effects are noted in the book "Alcoholics Anonymous:"

"The almost certain consequences that follow taking even a glass of beer do not crowd into the mind to deter us. If these thoughts occur, they are hazy and readily supplanted with the old threadbare idea that this time we shall handle ourselves like other people. There is a complete failure of the kind of defense that keeps one from putting his hand on a hot stove. The alcoholic may say to himself in the most casual way, "It won't burn me this time, so here's how!" Or perhaps he doesn't think at all." (Anonymous, 2001, p. 24).

In other words, the power of the addiction will typically override the *nocebo* effect within a brief span of time.

Although studies have not been conducted in this particular aspect of Addictions Therapy, more than 80 years of experience with alcoholics, and those otherwise addicted, and millions of recoveries from addictions, would severely tip the scale against any speculation that the spiritual aspect of recovery would be based on the *placebo* effect or any other type of *suggestive* power or conditioning. It would also preclude the use of attempts by clinicians to substitute a placebo for a genuine spiritual remedy. Certainly, some research shows that the placebo effect has credible powers and, in isolated individual instances, may bring about temporary recovery. However, on-the-whole, the powerful forces of addictions do not lend themselves to psycho-suggestive remedies. The internal soothing and comforting properties of addictions are vastly more powerful than any psychosomatic effect. Additionally, research indicates that *knowledge* that a placebo response is being attempted negates the effectiveness of the process. (Harvard Medical School, 3-2005).

Placebo effects are short-lived, addictions are life-long. Alcoholics, and otherwise addicted individuals, require not only a *Power* greater than themselves to help overcome their addictions, but a *Power greater than their addictions*. The suggestive power of placebos and nocebos pale dramatically in comparison. In speaking of the spiritual remedy, Dr. Silkworth stated:

"Frothy emotional appeal seldom suffices. The message which can interest and hold these alcoholic people must have depth and weight. In nearly all cases, their ideals must be grounded in a power greater than themselves, if they are to re-create their lives." (Anonymous, 2001, p. xxvi).

Does Prayer Work?

By its nature, the Spirituality of Addictions Counseling would necessitate that the client be encouraged to develop a personal form of communication with his or her *Higher Power*. Such *communication* is generally characterized as *prayer*. The use of prayer, meditation, and spiritual connectedness are discussed as *essential* in the original recovery programs that have proven themselves to be effective with alcoholics and those with other addictive disorders. This chapter attempted to address the efficacy of prayer by the review of recent scientific research into the power and effectiveness of prayer. Most research on the topic of intercessory prayer was conducted in an effort to determine prayer's helpfulness to patients undergoing surgery or those with specific illnesses other than addictions. The conclusion of this review of available research is that prayer is effective in certain instances. It also concludes that the number of variables involved in conducting any study on prayer is astronomical. As such, the inability of any study to effectively control for such variables brings its scientific results into question on the basis of reliability and validity. However, even though science has not yet discovered a way to reliably validate the miracles they observe, the miracles occur nonetheless. This topic is exceptionally interesting and warrants further inquiry.

Regardless of the outcome of any further studies, the evidence is clear that miracles through prayer have occurred, and continue to occur, in addictions recovery programs. These miracles are not, as some have speculated, the result of the placebo or nocebo effect. In other words, *the power of prayer is not based on the placebo effect.* Although the placebo and nocebo effects are considerable, they are not effective against addictions. Addictions are vastly more powerful than any such psychosomatic effect. Nevertheless, when the client, through observing its positive affects in others, also comes to *believe* in the spiritual solution contained in 12 Step programs and in the healing power of prayer, the placebo effect can strengthen and support their recovery. Prior to the inception of the spiritually based program of Alcoholics Anonymous, no religious, medical, or psychological method had ever proven effective in the treatment of alcoholism or other addictions. *If prayer and spiritual connectedness are not effective in the treatment of addictions, then the question remains: what element within these 12 Step programs is the primary factor in their overall rate of success?*

Does prayer work? Yes, but how, why, where, when, and with whom? These are variables that are not *humanly* answerable. 'God's' knowledge, mind, will, and one's personal relationship to the *"God of their own conception,"* are all factors in the outcome of prayer. Such factors are not able to be scientifically replicated. As such then, perhaps the best use of prayer is outlined in Step 11 which states:

"Sought through prayer and meditation to improve our conscious contact with God as we understood Him, praying only for knowledge of His will for us and the power to carry that out." (Anonymous, 2001, p. 59)

With Sobriety,
All Else
Is Possible

Chapter 14

New (Old) Considerations in Alcoholism and Addictions Recovery

Three-fold Disease Concept

Since its inception, Alcoholics Anonymous has made the determination that alcoholism is a *physical* (allergy), a *mental* (obsession), and a *spiritual* (malady). In an attempt to treat the most obvious symptoms of addiction, secular-scientific mental health clinicians (and all other types of helping professionals) naturally commenced work on *convincing* the alcoholic to stop drinking. However, centuries of various therapeutic interventions attempting to relieve alcoholics of their *obsession* to drink has proven, despite numerous repeated attempts, time and again to be frustrating, heartbreaking, and fruitless. (O'Neal, HS, 2011).

Spiritual Awakening in 12 Step Programs

The book "Alcoholics Anonymous" describes good doctors and psychiatrists, who were leading experts in the fields of alcoholism and drug addictions, as "exceedingly anxious to adopt" any method, of assisting their patients, "that *worked*." The work of these doctors involved the hospitalization of their clients to *physically* separate them from alcohol and/or drugs, and psychotherapy to alleviate their *mental obsession* to drink or use. When early members of Alcoholics

Anonymous approached these doctors with a request to talk to the alcoholic patients in their facilities with the hope of bringing A.A. into these institutions, the doctors agreed. However, as a trial, they selected some of the most hopeless alcoholics from among their patients for test cases. The doctors wanted to test the claims of recovery carried by these early members of Alcoholics Anonymous. These men from A.A. claimed that they themselves were also once hopeless, but through this newly discovered spiritually based program, recovery from alcoholism had become possible for them, and for many of the others they had shared it with. Following the success of this initial test, the spiritual program of Alcoholics Anonymous was brought into these hospitals and was well received - *because it offered a solution that worked!* With experience as criterion, more than half of those who were exposed to A.A. became members and began the process of permanent recovery. (Anonymous, 2001, pp. xxiv, xxvii, 7, 11, 20, 163).

From this example it can be seen that the secular-scientific based medical and psychiatric approaches, which are designed to engage and treat only the physical and mental symptoms of addictions, have proven to be ineffective in alleviating the observable symptoms of addictions. They are also ineffective in assisting clients to achieve and maintain long term sobriety. However, when the spiritual approach is employed, the majority of those who accept this method of treatment will experience *physical*, *mental,* and *spiritual* recovery. "When the spiritual malady is overcome, we straighten out mentally and physically." (Anonymous, 2001, pp. xxv, 14, 64)

Prior to Alcoholics Anonymous, occasional miraculous recoveries were documented when an alcoholic experienced what was known as a *vital spiritual experience*. These spiritually based recoveries were rare and health practitioners were not able to predict or explain when, why, or how such events would occur, or even 'if' they would occur in, or for, any particular client. Even when such events were observed by helping professionals, those clinicians were at a loss to replicate such recoveries in others. (Jung, 1961). As precursors to A.A., the Washingtonians (1840) and the Oxford Groups (1922) began seeing successful results in the remission of alcoholism through an organization of God-centered, pseudo-religious, fellowships that provided a structured program of recovery and ongoing mutual support. However, disagreements over *religious* issues and *leadership* led to their demise. It wasn't until the advent in 1935 of the spiritually oriented program and fellowship of Alcoholics Anonymous that '*a*' working method of achieving and sustaining long-term recovery was introduced (Breining, et al., 2008).

While its effectiveness was evident, and although it recognized and defined alcoholism as a physical disease, Alcoholics Anonymous was only able to address the *mental obsession* and *spiritual malady* aspects of the ailment of alcoholism. Nevertheless, A.A. members rightly observed that *through abstinence*, the *physical allergy* aspect of the disease was also arrested. It was only when the alcoholic took *the first drink* that the *allergy* was again awakened. At this point, the *allergic reaction* prompted the "*phenomenon of craving*" in the alcoholic, which then blotted out all normal reasoning. And, although the alcoholic's desire was only to return to 'normal' drinking, relapse into full alcoholic symptoms, that were more severe than those that drove them to try to stop drinking in the first place, *always* seemed to ensue. Following the resumption of drinking, within a very short period of time, it was as though they had never stopped drinking. Periods of abstinence offered no lessening in the symptoms of the disease. Hence, entire abstinence was determined to be the initial crucial aspect of recovery.

Prior to, and even in spite of, these aspects of the disease concept of alcoholism, as delineated by Alcoholics Anonymous, secular-scientific researchers and therapists continued to view people who had developed addictions, not as people with a disease, but rather as people who were "morally flawed," "lacking in will power," and/or capable of normal living if only they would "break the habit and drink normally." Recently however, research has lead the secular-scientific medical community to concur with the findings of Alcoholics Anonymous and recognize that an *"addiction is a chronic disease that changes both the brain structure and function, just as cardiovascular disease changes the heart."* (Harvard Medical School, 7-2011).

As Alcoholics Anonymous has always professed, scientists are now concluding that scientific remedies designed to alleviate the symptoms of addictions through short-term solutions, are insufficient to bring about the desired results. The complexity and effects of alcoholism and other addictive disorders on the body and brain are so profound that any short-term remedy is precluded. That despite drug therapy, placebo therapy, psychoanalysis, cognitive-behavioral therapy, clinical group interventions, etc., the treatment of the disease of alcoholism and other addictions will not, over time, yield to any single secular approach for remediation. Additionally, any seemingly effective short-term remediation is doomed to eventually fail in that addictions are life-long and will require continuous ongoing interventions in order for the client to remain symptom free. (Harvard Medical School, 7-2005).

Once convinced that they have an addiction, patients sometimes inquire if a spiritual approach is necessary for their recovery. A response to this question is described in the book "Alcoholics Anonymous:" "Whether such a person can quit upon a nonspiritual basis depends upon the extent to which he has already lost the power to choose..." If the client has tried and found it "impossible to stop drinking" [or using], "no matter how great the necessity or wish," then they are more than likely beyond the tipping point where recovery on a non-spiritual basis can prove effective. (Anonymous, 2001, p. 34). Experiential history has shown that the non-religious, spiritual concepts presented in the program of Alcoholics Anonymous are not, and need not be, socially invasive in their lives, but rather are simple, individual, and personal to the member.

Doctors have learned that clients who are active in Alcoholics Anonymous display genuine improvement. One study states: "Today we know that alcoholism and other addictions are chronic illnesses... which require long-term self-management and pervasive and consistent changes in the way a person lives. The discipline and fellowship of A.A. are valuable for many alcoholics because they fulfill that function in a way no other treatment can." (Harvard Medical School, 7-2007). Although the statements from the cited study are technically accurate, it must be emphasized that A.A. does not 'discipline' any member or compel any member to make any changes or take any actions. Alcoholics Anonymous is strictly a voluntary program. Although certain actions are usually necessary to better ensure continued recovery, these actions, such as taking the 12 steps, are suggested and encouraged, but are never required.

Newer members in Alcoholics Anonymous are encouraged to look for other members who have more experience in the program, someone with whom they feel comfortable and can trust. When they find such an individual, it is suggested that they ask that person to help *sponsor*, or guide them through their program of recovery. This process is mutually beneficial in that the member providing the guidance is fulfilling his or her role in the 12th step. The member providing the guidance is attempting to be of maximum service to the newer member, and as such, to 'God.' The benefit these members receive by 'giving' is to *get out of self* and experience the joy of humbly and gratefully being of service to another human being. In-so-doing, this 'being of service to others' helps safeguard their own continued recovery. Additionally, as members *live* the *spiritual service* aspects of 12 Step programs, their lives often begin to thrive. Their personas take on a certain positive, friendly glow and they begin to gain inner strength. Newer members are attracted to this confidence and positive outlook. As such, the newer member will begin to *want* what the more seasoned members *have* with regard to serenity, inner strength, and overall quality of life.

Once the newer member begins to *see* that those more seasoned members are actually practicing the program themselves and are getting observable results, then the newer member begins to gain *faith* in the process and becomes *willing* to *do* what the more seasoned members *have done* to achieve and maintain their own sobriety. A saying is: "If you want what we have, come and do what we do." The new member then is ready to take the steps designed for their recovery. These suggested, *spiritually oriented*, steps only work if taken voluntarily by one who is ready and willing to take them.

The *Spiritual Awakening* aspect of 12 Step programs is stated to have been achieved during the process of taking the steps. Step 12 states: "Having had a spiritual awakening as the result of these steps, we tried to carry this message to alcoholics, and to practice these principles in all our affairs." (Anonymous, 2001, p. 60). Part of the spiritual aspect of Step 12 is that when members are working with newer members in an attempt to help them achieve, maintain, and sustain sobriety, the older members voluntarily become accountable to their 'God' and to the other person. The more seasoned members maintain their own sobriety, in part, to be available to their newfound friends and assist them through the recovery process.

As more seasoned members work with newer members they begin to realize that they have become more concerned with the welfare of another human being than they are with *self*. They realize that their care for another is genuine, that their own lives have become richer and more full for having had the experience, and that they are, without consciously doing so, growing closer to 'God.' They grow closer to 'God' when they recognize that it was the *Spirit* of 'God' operating *through* them that provided the *Power* to bring recovery into the life of a newer member. This knowledge, that it was the *Power* of the *Spirit* at work in the newer member, and not any power within themselves, that the more seasoned member begins to understand the meaning of genuine usefulness and humility. Ego rightly diminishes. Often, relationships such as these become lifelong friendships, both with the member and with 'God.' Soon too, with the assistance of those who helped them, the once new members begin to share their experience with other newer members.

Growing Medical Involvement in Recovery Treatment Programs

As noted previously, since its founding, Alcoholics Anonymous defined alcoholism as a disease and advocated for its appropriate treatment by medical and psychiatric authorities. Other addictions were later also classified as addictive diseases and were found to respond positively to spiritually based 12 Step programs as well. Recently, within the last 15 years, medical science has also concluded that "alcoholism is a physical disease which requires continuing medical treatment." Medical practitioners are becoming increasingly convinced that alcoholism is not merely "a problem in the sufferer's head – something that can be overcome through willpower, spirituality, or talk therapy." Previously, the medical establishment assigned alcoholism and other addictions to a far corner of the medical realm relegated only within the purview of the psychiatrist. Today however, the medical establishment is embracing the original assertion that alcoholism is a *disease* and, as such, alcoholism is *a physical diagnosis* instead of a *mental* one.

On July 1, 2011, the medical profession launched "its first accredited residency program in *Addiction Medicine* where doctors who have completed medical school and a primary residency will be able to spend a year studying the relationship between addiction and brain chemistry." "The goal of the residency program is to establish Addiction Medicine as a standard specialty along the lines of pediatrics, oncology or dermatology." "The Residents will study and treat a wide "range of addictions," "brain chemistry," and the role of heredity." Once fully established and "accredited in a minimum of 20 institutions, the '*Addictions*' specialty would qualify as a '*primary*' residency program."

With the redefinition of alcoholism and other addictive disorders as *medical* rather than *psychological* conditions, treatments will be altered to encompass a greater array of pharmaceuticals in combination with therapy. Additionally, recognition of addictions as a *physical disease* brings the belief that, just as diabetes is a physical disease that requires continuous treatment, treatment for addictions must be ongoing as well in order to avoid relapse. (Quenqua, 2011). Although 12 Step programs are included in the treatment aspect for most addictions, pharmaceuticals appear to be well suited to assist greatly in the treatment of opiates and derivatives thereof. An article on genetic predisposition and etiology of addictions discussed heredity factors of certain addictions and the addictive properties of certain chemicals which have no familial connectivity. However, their etiologies will bear significantly on the type and nature of the treatments likely to produce lasting remission of symptoms. (O'Neal, HS, 2011). Nevertheless, regardless of the causation of addiction, and irrespective of the interventions prescribed, the attitude and "personality change sufficient enough to bring about recovery" from addiction (Anonymous, 2001, p. apdx II) has proven to be a connection to, and conscious contact with, a *Spiritual Power* greater than both the client and the addiction. Such a *personality change* will generally enhance the therapeutic value of any and all prescribed remedies.

Alcoholics Anonymous claims to have no monopoly on recovery and no monopoly on 'God.' Also, it has always cooperated widely with practitioners of medicine and religion (Anonymous, 2001, pp. xx, xxi, 95). It is interesting that, as the medical establishment begins to fully recognize the physical aspect of alcoholism and other addictive disorders, and begins to lay claim to diagnostic primacy and oversight in the treatment of addictions, the role and function the medical profession should play in the field of addictions treatment was delineated in 1939 in the book "Alcoholics Anonymous." The book discussed the role of medical practitioners in the secular, non-spiritual, care and treatment of those in recovery. The book also predicted that it was 'God' who would provide alcoholics with these secular practitioners and caretakers:

"We are convinced that a spiritual mode of living is a most powerful health restorative. We, who have recovered from serious drinking, are miracles of mental health. But we have seen remarkable transformations in our bodies. Hardly one of our crowd now shows any mark of dissipation.

But this does not mean that we disregard human health measures. God has abundantly supplied this world with fine doctors, psychologists, and practitioners of various kinds. Do not hesitate to take your health problems to such persons. Most of them give freely of themselves, that their fellows may enjoy sound minds and   bodies. Try to remember that though God has wrought miracles among us, we should never belittle a good doctor or psychiatrist. Their services are often indispensable in treating a newcomer and in following his case afterward." (Anonymous, 2001, p. 133).

What was understood by the authors of the book "Alcoholics Anonymous" was that the individual members, and the 'program' of A.A., would be the institution responsible to provide *continuing lifelong care and intervention for those in recovery*. Those in the medical profession could "follow his case afterward," but they are not equipped, nor designed to provide, the lifelong therapeutic care required by recovering alcoholics and individuals possessed with other addictive disorders. Bill W., co-founder of Alcoholics Anonymous discussed who should be 'responsible' for ensuring such continuing care was available for those in need. He indicated that A.A. should always be available to anyone who reaches out for help. And, he related that as a member of A.A., *he* was responsible for ensuring that such help was continually available. His words were: "I am responsible." His words inspire those who adhere to the A.A. program to also take personal responsibility for assisting those who seek help for their alcoholism. Other 12 Step programs, that follow the *spiritual* principles of A.A., typically provide similar assistance to those in need.

With Sobriety,

All Else

Is Possible

Chapter 15

Summary and Conclusions

The definitions of *Spirituality* encompass a broad spectrum of concepts. For the purposes of this book, *Spirituality* is utilized in the context of the individual client's own conception of a "Higher Power," or of a 'God' unique to them. The spiritual 'God' or "Higher Power" concept is noted to be the primary healing *Power* and restorative element in Alcoholics Anonymous. This 'God' concept was the centerpiece, or "The Solution," indicated as the regenerative *power* needed for healing the disease of alcoholism and restoring the lives of suffers. The healing appears to be attributable to the client gaining access to and connection with a "Power Greater than themselves." Although this connectivity with a Spiritual Power Greater than one's self very frequently produces observable, positive, and even miraculous results, scientifically identifying and replicating this *power* remains elusive. Thus far, harnessing this *power* for use in a clinical therapeutic environment under scientific conditions has proven equally elusive. Nevertheless, though elusive, this *power* is undeniably present and consistently produces comparably effective results in clients.

Secular-scientific, non-spiritual, practitioners believe that if they cannot define, dissect, measure, recreate, and reproduce a specific spiritual condition, even though they can observe its effects, then they disregard its results as mere coincidence or anomalous. Because the anomaly is outside of their understanding, they deem its origins and effects as being derived through superstition or other causations such as a psychosomatic effect based suggestion, placebo, etc. Nevertheless, despite science's inability to accurately define or prove the existence of the *Spirit* in spiritually based therapy, such therapy exists in the Addictions Counseling field, where the *experience* of its clients, has proven it to be exceptionally effective. The success of the spiritually based recovery method, in the once bleak and hopeless field of Addictions Therapy, has ignited the interest of all who have witnessed it.

Other numerous and varied therapeutic models have attempted to assist alcoholics and those with other addictive disorders overcome their dependencies. Some have achieved encouraging successes. However, those successes are typically short lived. Neither before, nor since the advent of Alcoholics Anonymous in 1935, has any non-spiritual method of recovery been able to achieve the lasting success rates that have been realized through the *spiritual* approach to recovery.

This book has endeavored to examine available research literature in order to explore the effectiveness of spiritually based counseling. This research was conducted in order to determine if there are any significant differences in effectiveness between spiritually based practices and other major approaches to counseling. As much as practicable, the examination of these approaches was geared toward their effectiveness within the arena of Addictions Counseling. After discovering the suspected underlying problem, the goal in most therapeutic counseling procedures is the reduction of presenting symptoms.

Conversely, the goal of counseling in treating most areas of addiction (with obvious notable exceptions), is total abstinence. As such, the initial measurement of the effectiveness of any addictions treatment methodology is the length of sustained abstinence achieved by clients. Therefore, the primary goal of Addictions Counseling is the life-long, continuous abstinence of the client from addictive substances or behaviors. Additionally, the goal of any addictions treatment program or philosophy is for the client to abstain from essentially *all* forms of addiction and *all* mood altering substances with the exception of those medically prescribed. The reason for total abstention is that clients with addictive disorders will substitute one addiction for another, which in turn, will eventually lead clients to revert back to their original presenting addiction.

Three primary approaches to counseling were reviewed. The three treatment approach types were: Secular-Scientific, Religious-Biblical, and Spiritual. The key factors discovered, in which these approaches differ, proved to be the deciding elements critical to their effectiveness for assisting those who suffer from addictions. Those key elements were: the *goal and objective of therapy, the role of the counselor,* and the *source of power* required to achieve the aims of counseling. In most instances, alcoholism and other addictions are viewed as the symptoms to the underlying problems of the client. However, once the client has crossed-the-line into addiction, abstinence of addictive behavior becomes paramount to any therapy addressing underlying difficulties. Certainly other disorders can be treated concurrently. However, the priority for treatment should be the client's addiction. The reason the client's addiction should take precedence over other issues is because, if the client should return to addictive behaviors, the addiction is likely to negate any previous progress made in therapy for any other underlying disorder. The return of addictive behavior usually renders any future continuing treatment meaningless, unless the client re-achieves abstinence. This is because the addiction will retake supremacy in the life of the client.

Secular-Scientific Approach

Secular-Scientific: The *goal* of counseling in the secular-scientific approach is to help the client understand the emotions behind his or her addiction and contemplate reducing addictive behaviors. The *objective* of therapy in the secular-scientific approach is harmony with *self*. The *power* source tapped to provide recovery is that power found within the client. The counselor or therapist may feel that they possess the power within themselves to 'treat' the client and, based on their training and experience, that may be the case. However, that *power* is ultimately only available to them at the discretion of the client. In other words, only in-so-far-as the client *believes* that the counselor possesses therapeutic power does the counselor possess that power.

In this approach, the *role of the counselor* is to 'affirm' the client. As the counselor is successful in 'affirming' the client, the client should 'feel' harmony-within-self. Regardless of whether or not the client's behaviors or emotions are appropriate or within societal norms, as long as the client 'feels' affirmed - that their thoughts and/or actions are appropriate - then the client *feels* justified, powerful, and in charge of their own destiny. If successful, the client feels empowered, but attributes their gain of that empowerment to the therapeutic skill of the secular therapist. They will then look to the counselor to help them control their newfound power within. Thus, the client perceives the counselor as the one with the *power* and projects that power into the counselor. *When the client's addiction is more powerful than the power projected into the counselor by the client, then the goal of abstinence in Addictions Therapy fails.* However, in the event that *if* the client is able to achieve and maintain sobriety, or abstinence from their addiction, *then* therapy will be required to continue indefinitely if any chance of sustained abstinence is to be possible. Addictions are life-long. As such, for those truly addicted, some form of readily available, ongoing, therapeutic intervention is necessary.

Religious-Biblical Approach

Religious - Biblical: The *goal* of counseling in this approach is to seek divine assistance in the cessation of an addiction or an addictive behavior. The *objective* of the religious-biblical approach to therapy is to: recognize one's sinful nature, examination of conscience, confession of sins, and the seeking of redemption from eternal punishment. The 'God' recognized by the particular religious faith or denomination is the 'God' who holds the *Power* necessary for the client to achieve the goal and objective of therapy. The *counselor* is viewed as a knowledgeable facilitator whose *role* it is to assist the client in reconciliation with the 'God' of the Bible, or the 'God' of the particular religious denominational dogma recognized by both the counselor and the client.

In Addictions Counseling, the elements in the religious approach are not incompatible with sustained recovery from addiction. Typically affiliation with a church or other religious institution may assist the client with maintaining an ongoing relationship with God. Ongoing support groups and regular church activities throughout the week are beneficial for those in remission from addictive disorders. Thus, the client may be able to maintain continuous abstinence from their addiction. Nevertheless, a drawback of this approach, particularly for those with significant addictions, is *the feeling of being guided into a commitment with an external institutional God of someone else's understanding.* A disagreement with a minister, (who perhaps is unfamiliar with addictions), a change in pastors, moving to another church, changing denominational affiliation, or an alteration in the tone of the religious environment, may disrupt the client's perception of 'God.' Such changes may alter the client's relationship(s) within the institution and thus disturb the client's internal harmony to such a degree that it spurs a relapse into addictions or addictive behaviors. This relapse may be due to the client viewing the religious institution as their source of restorative power rather than the *power* of a 'God' personal to him or herself.

Spiritual Approach

Spiritual: The *goal* of therapy within the spiritual counseling approach is the immediate achievement of abstinence from addictive behaviors. The *objective* of therapy is for clients to come into a state of being at one with, or of being in harmony with, the 'Spirit of the Universe,' or the 'God' of their *own* conception. In this approach, general counseling techniques are utilized in an eclectic manner from other sources and are tailored toward the individual client's current situation. As in the religious-biblical approach, the therapeutic *power* necessary for the client to achieve the goal of abstinence, is 'God.' But it is 'God' as perceived by the *client*. The *role* of the clinician is to act as a guide in steering the client to a greater understanding of, and submission to, his or her own "Higher Power" – his or her *own conception* of 'God.' *This 'God' is not only more powerful than the client, but more powerful than the client's addiction.* Attainment of abstinence from the client's addiction, and more importantly, the client's *continued* abstinence from addiction, is dependent on the *daily maintenance* of a *spiritual* connection with the client's own conception of '*God.*'

One way this spiritual connectivity can be accomplished is by practicing the principles of Alcoholics Anonymous or other related recovery program. If these principles are practiced, clients will begin to feel in harmony with their 'God.' Conversely, if they start to move away from 'God,' they will begin to feel out of harmony or out-of-tune with Him. If their thoughts or actions are not in keeping with the principles by which they are attempting to live, clients will begin to feel agitated, isolated, disgruntled, and angry. These feelings of discontentment will continue and grow stronger until the client takes the actions necessary to bring him or herself back into harmony with 'God.' The more this process is instilled and emphasized in the client, the more likely continuous abstinence will be sustained.

With continued abstinence and increasing harmony with 'God,' the greater the probability that the client's life will see rapid positive growth. This growth will be evidenced by a greater ability to resolve conflicts, a greater orientation toward personal achievement, an improvement in health, a more positive emotional outlook, attainment of a feeling of usefulness and purpose based on providing service to others, gaining a sense of joy and personal fulfillment, etc. Additionally, the spiritual approach to counseling may have the complimentary effect of bringing the client to a closer understanding of previously held religious beliefs, or may encourage the client to seek 'God' in a more formal religious setting. However, caution should be used to ensure that the client does not lose his or her spiritual groundedness and thus possibly lose sobriety. People who have known the restorative power of the *Spirit*, and experienced that *Power's* incredible healing and forgiveness, often seek to further their understanding of 'God' through some form of religious inquiry. This tendency is perhaps an attempt to better understand the nature of the *Spirit* that they have discovered within themselves. A significant aspect of recovery is continuing *spiritual* growth.

A Counseling Technique for Finding 'God'

This book examined spiritually based counseling techniques. Those techniques won't be reviewed here with the exception of the simple but very effective religious based approach noted by Dr. Ian Jones (Jones, 2006). Dr. Jones utilizes Biblical references to help aid in the understanding of the relationship between the Biblical God and Man, and to illustrate how the counselor might better assist the client in finding a direction to the *restorative power* of God. Dr. Jones' method lends itself nicely to being tailored to spiritually based Addictions Counseling. His philosophy is essentially what he terms as a "location" and a "call." From "Genesis," the first book of the Bible, after "the fall of man," God poses the question of *location* to Adam: "Where are you?" And, from "Revelation," the last book of the Bible, God invites or *calls* for mankind to "Come" to receive Him.

From these concepts then, the *direction* necessary to reach God comes into focus. Extrapolated from these, a therapist using the spiritual approach would first determine the client's conception of 'God.' Once established, the counselor then inquires of the client *where* they feel they are in relation to their 'God,' thus establishing the direction and distance the client needs to travel in order to come into conscious contact with his or her 'God.' Action is then required on the part of the client to follow the path necessary to meet and remain in harmony with 'God.' Essentially this counselor assisted process is designed to aid the client to: 1) Define their 'God'; 2) Determine where '*self*' is in relation to this 'God' (direction to 'God'); and 3) Begin moving toward 'God' (distance to 'God'). This growth process of moving in the direction of, and ever closer to 'God,' is a lifelong *spiritual journey*.

Placebo & Nocebo Effect, the Effectiveness of Prayer, and New Medical Considerations

Other considerations worthy of discussion, related to the topic of *Spirituality* as the healing *Power* in Addictions Counseling, were the placebo/nocebo effects; the effectiveness of prayer; and the newly instituted concept within the medical profession of viewing alcoholism and other addictive disorders as a medical (physical) diagnosis. The placebo effect and prayer were both addressed in order to examine their possible effect on, and relationship to each other, and to the spiritual approach. As a medical diagnosis, *addictions* are deemed to be treatable with prescription medications instead of a condition for which a more psychological approach is taken. Implications of this concept were explored.

Under certain conditions placebos and nocebos have been proven to play a powerful role in the physical and mental health of certain individuals. This effect is based on numerous, usually suggestive, factors. Spirituality, and the power of prayer, has sometimes been construed as being the result of the psychological influence of suggestion. This book reviewed these effects and determined that, although powerful suggestive cognitive forces were evident in placebos and nocebos, such effects were easily negated in the alcoholic and in those with other addictive disorders, in that *once the nature of a placebo is known, it loses its power* - and, *the lasting nature of, and forces behind addictions, are vastly superior in power and prevalence to any effect that might be produced from a placebo or nocebo.* As such, if the spiritual approach to recovery from addictions were nothing more than the effect produced by a placebo, then 12 Step programs, including Alcoholics Anonymous, would only have had a brief existence before becoming yet another failed attempt at solving the age old riddle of alcoholism and other addictions. The *spiritual solution* contained in these programs has proven to be the powerful *change-agent* necessary to bring about recovery from alcoholism and other addictive disorders.

This book also explored the power of prayer. Several research studies on the topic of prayer were examined with mixed results. The studies typically dealt with *intercessory prayer* in which a patient's recovery was prayed for by others. There were numerous variables in these studies that called their reliability and validity into question. However, in a general way, the results of these studies provide valuable information for future research. Some studies show a positive correlation between prayer and improved medical patient outcomes, while others showed little to no correlation. With the amount of variables involved, these results are not surprising. The studies which displayed the strongest positive correlations tended to have fewer variables. Nevertheless, groups of individuals who regularly practice intercessory prayer for others, contend that they have observed miracles that they feel are directly attributable to prayer. They indicated that despite science's less than positive study findings on the effectiveness of intercessory prayer, they have no intention of stopping.

Antithetical to intercessory prayer, studies examining *personal prayer* displayed significantly more positive results. Prayer, as used here, and for the research studies examined, was not so much delineated in specific form or format, but rather the term *prayer* is used to denote any form whereby the participant communicated with the 'God' of his or her own understanding. In virtually every case, a significant positive outcome was noted wherein an individual professed closeness to, or a conscious spiritual contact with, his or her own conception of 'God.'

Achievement of this type of personal contact with one's Creator is the essence of spiritual experience. This humble conscious relationship is noted to be *the restorative Power* described in the book "Alcoholics Anonymous." These studies corroborate the effectiveness of this type of prayerful relationship with a Power Greater than Oneself.

Spiritual Recovery

The Spiritual Approach to recovery has made life livable for countless alcoholics, and those with other addictions. More often than not, when these people are introduced to 12 Step programs, they typically possess few common skills for living or for coping with everyday life. Their addiction was the solution to all their problems. Once sober, clean, and/or no longer performing their addictive behavior(s), they realize that they possess very few of the 'tools,' or coping mechanisms, that are generally necessary to deal with the emotional ups and downs of everyday 'real life.' Clients who have adopted a spiritual mode of living often find that besides removing their addictive obsessions, their *faith* in their "Higher Power," and their *willingness* to follow *spiritual principles*, will help them solve their other life issues as well.

Continuing Support

Much in this book will lead the reader to the conclusion that it is suggesting the counselor steer their clients toward attendance in Alcoholics Anonymous, or to another 12 step program. Indeed counselors who provide such guidance may be assured that if their clients fully engage themselves in such programs they will have a system of support continually available to help them with their needs. However, there are other means of support available that may provide the continuing assistance clients will require following completion of their counseling regimen and their initial remission from their addiction. The therapist should research and explore all such options and present them to their clients as they near completion of their treatment program. However, most such programs are either not spiritually based, or are religiously based. Other factors, such as *availability* need to be considered as well. The following paragraph delineates some of the benefits 12 Step programs offer. Counselors should compare the benefits offered in other long-term aftercare programs to those inherently available in 12 Step programs.

Continual support is necessary for those with addictions in that addictions are life-long. Therefore, lifelong support is typically necessary in order to keep addictions in remission. 12 Step programs have been primarily discussed here as resources of choice. 12 Step programs are typically preferred for aftercare in that over time they have: 1) Proven to be effective; 2) Are generally available worldwide; 3) In larger areas, they are available every day of the week – and often several times during the day; 4) There is no obligation to the client; 5) They are anonymous; and 6) There is no cost to participate. Other available continuing treatment programs usually do not have these same advantages and are not, as of yet, suitably prevalent. However, at times, other types of after-care programs are beneficial when used in combination with 12 Step programs. As such, in the best interest of their clients and to help them prevent relapse, counselors should ensure that clients are familiar with all available resources in order to assist them with continuing personal and spiritual growth. All such programs should be researched, visited, and explored with the client. To ensure transition, active engagement in a preferred aftercare program should be commenced prior to exiting the client from counseling services.

_____*****_____

In discussing his experiences with the *Spiritual* aspect of recovery, a member of Alcoholics Anonymous was recently heard to share that his alcoholism had taken him to the very depths of hell. He related that he had been spared destruction by the powerful hand of 'God.' In describing his initial feelings of recovery, he said that he likened his journey into hell as similar to that portrayed in Dante's "Inferno." He said that just prior to his miraculous recovery, while in the morass of drunken despair, he had a dream. He said he dreamed that he was being forced to trudge down a steep winding pathway into the blistering fires of hell. He said that on his descent into the hellish pit he passed under an archway which bore an inscription which read: "Abandon All Hope Ye Who Enter Here." He said feelings of hopelessness and despair swept over him as he was forced to trudge deeper into the scorching flames.

Then, in a moment of absolute agony and despair, he fell to his knees and cried out: "Oh God, please help me!" Instantly, he said he heard what sounded like a *wind* behind him. He turned and saw the hand of God stretching itself down the path. Reaching through the arch it grabbed him, *turned him around*, and placed him on the path leading upward. Fatigued but happy, he began the long assent up out of the depths of hades. The path was steep and the work of climbing hard, but he was filled with gratitude for his redemption and deliverance. As he again approached the arch, through the smoke and ash he realized that there was an inscription on the reverse side of it too. Having been in hell's fires, and realizing that he had just been miraculously spared eternity there, tears filled his eyes as he described the emotions he felt when he again passed under the arch and read the inscription there. The inscription read: "Welcome to Alcoholics Anonymous." (H., Doug, 2011).

_____*****_____

With Sobriety,
All Else
Is Possible

Epilogue

When clients have overcome the initial throes of their addiction and appear to have come into conscious contact with the 'God' of their own conception, their lives begin to show signs of significant progress. There are often restored relationships, improved financial situations, offers of new opportunities, a myriad of seemingly complex problems begin to fade, etc., and life for the client and their significant others begins to show bright promise for the future. Family, friends, employers, clergy, counselors, etc. begin to breathe a collective sigh of relief that their friend, loved-one, client, or employee has seemingly overcome their addiction. As the client's life continues to improve, loved ones and friends begin to divert their attention elsewhere. The person with the addiction begins to feel that 'the pressure is off' and life is returning to 'normal.' But, what was previously 'normal,' is no longer so. What is 'normal?'

It must always be remembered that *it is the addicted individual's responsibility to maintain his or her own sobriety and to be engaged in his or her own recovery program*. Nevertheless, alcoholism, and other addictive disorders, has affected all who interact with those who are afflicted. They have also been, in a sense, 'broken' in their reaction to life. Conversely, all concerned parties should be knowledgeable of, and engaged in, the ongoing process of recovery. As friends, family, therapists, etc. begin to become less vigilant of the client's behaviors; they are no longer singularly focused on the client and tend to relax their vigilance of the client's activities. They become less and less weary, more trusting, and begin to welcome the client back into the general routine of life. They let down their emotional guard and begin to treat the client with greater trust, kindness, and compassion. This is all well and good, and a natural response. But often the client, still relatively new in recovery, views such trust and passivity as an excuse or permission to reduce their prescribed recovery program activities and/or counseling regimen.

As the routines and rigors of 'normal' life return, the client may begin to do things like skip counseling sessions, miss regular aftercare meetings, begin to deviate from their recommended program, etc. There may be reasonable excuses for doing so at first, but soon this behavior may start to become habitual. Unfortunately, all too often, well-meaning family members, friends - and counselors too - may subconsciously sabotage the client's recovery program with comments such as: "Oh, you're doing great! You don't need to go to those meetings anymore;" "Yeah, I know you've had some problems, but you weren't that bad, you're doing so well, you may not really be an alcoholic;" "When are you going to graduate from that A.A. thing?" "Oh honey, our friends invited us to dinner tonight. I know you missed your meetings last week. What's the harm in missing another one?" etc., etc.

Unfortunately, although the client has made tremendous external progress, has made assurances of continued abstinence and reassured with sweet, heartfelt promises of a new and altered lifestyle, it is often the case that when the 'heat is off,' and the major obstacles in their lives are being overcome, the 'obsession' to return to their addiction oriented mode of living often comes on strong. At this point the client may succumb to temptation and relapse. This is often done without premeditated thought. A friend or family member may innocently offer the client a drink at a party, and the client takes it. There are any number of seemingly non-threatening scenarios that may lead the client to take the 'first' drink. Although it's the client's responsibility to manage their own sobriety, having recently heard a well-meaning friend or loved one say: "Well, maybe you're not really an alcoholic," may prompt a response of "Sure, why not? I'll have that drink." There often appears to be no thought of the tragic consequences of previous episodes, nor recall of their recent struggles to gain sobriety and restore lives, livelihood, and family. It just feels 'normal.' They suffer from a disease that tells them they don't have a disease. The insanity of the cycle of addiction returns.

A warning of this 'cycle' for the alcoholic is found in the book "Alcoholics Anonymous." It describes this process for the alcoholic, [which may be generally extrapolated for those with other addictive disorders], as such:

> "It is easy to let up on the *spiritual program of action* and rest on our laurels. We are headed for trouble if we do, for alcohol is a subtle foe. We are not cured of alcoholism. What we really have is a *daily reprieve contingent on the maintenance of our spiritual condition.* Every day is a day when we must carry the vision of God's will into all of our activities. "How can I best serve Thee- Thy will (not mine) be done." (*emphasis added*)
> (Anonymous, p. 85)

For those with addictions, the spiritual solution involves a change in lifestyle that incorporates conscious daily contact with the client's own conception of a Power Greater than themselves.

Counselors should encourage family members and friends of their addicted clients to investigate programs that are oriented to assist those with codependency issues. Codependency is typically the result of living and/or interacting with those with addictions.

Such programs may include, but are not limited to, "Al-Anon Family Groups" (AFG) and "Co-Dependents Anonymous" (CoDA). Information on Al-Anon family groups and Alateen may be found online at: al-anon.org. Information on Co-Dependents Anonymous may be found online at: coda.org. These and other related programs can provide information and support that will greatly assist all who have been affected by those with addictions. The principles contained in these programs are useful in providing a sound foundation on which to build strong and lasting relationships with self and others.

Additionally, clients with addictions rarely comprehend the nature of their own addictive disorder nor do they fully appreciate the effect their addictions have, and have had, on those around them, counselors included. As such, clinicians and other professionals who work with clients with addictions may also inadvertently find themselves in codependent relationships with their clients. Therapists may not fully comprehend that, more often than not, clinical work with those with addictions, is *counterintuitive* to the natural interpersonal inclinations of those in the helping professions.

There are many sources of information available to clinicians to assist them in this area of concern. Initially, counselors may do well to investigate the same organizations previously noted for friends and family members of those with addictions. A further source of information may be found in the author's article: "Codependency among health care professionals: Is an understanding of codependency issues important to the therapeutic counseling process?" (O'Neal, H., 2011) This article is available online in the *Journal of Addictive Disorders*. The book "Alcoholics Anonymous" is also an excellent source of reference for all affected parties. It may be viewed or obtained online at: aa.org.

References

American Psychiatric Association. (2000). *Diagnostic and Statistical Manual of Mental Disorders, Fourth Edition*. American Psychiatric Association.

Anonymous. (2001). *Alcoholics Anonymous* (4th ed.). New York City: Alcoholics Anonymous World Services, Inc.

BBC News. (2003, October 15). 'No health benefit' from prayer. *BBC News*.

BBC News. (2005, July 15). Prayer 'no aid to heart patients' . *BBC News*.

Beecher, H. K. (1955). The Powerful Placebo. *Journal of the American Medical Association, 159*(17), 1602-1606.

Benedict XVI, P. (2011, June 30). *Papal Address to Ratzinger Prize Winners "The Real Question": "Is What We Believe True or Not?"*. Retrieved July 3, 2011, from Zenit.org: http://www.zenit.org/article-32987?l=english

Blanch, A. (2007). Integrating Religion and Spirituality in Mental Health: The Promise and the Challenge. *Psychiatric Rehabilitation Journal, 30*(4), 251-260.

Breining, B. G., Anderson, S. T., Breining, M. J., Brown-Lidsey, V., Dakai, S. H., Ganaway, J., et al. (2008). *Addiction Professional; Manual for Counselor Competency* (Second ed.). Orangevale, California, United States of America: Breining Institute.

Bryner, J. (2010, December 14). *Prayer Relieves Mind in Many Ways, Study Finds*. Retrieved August 8, 2011, from Live Science: http://www.livescience.com/10889-prayer-relieves-mind-ways-study-finds.html

Corey, G. S.-C. (2007). *Issues and Ethics in the Helping Professions.* Belmont: Brooks/Cole.

DiClemente, C. S. (2004, March-April). Readiness and stages of change in addiciton treatment. *American Journal of Addiction, 13*(2), 103-119.

Duke University Medicine. (2006, October 17). *Friends in High Places*. Retrieved August 6, 2011, from DukeHealth.org: http://www.dukehealth.org/health_library/health_articles/friends_in_high_places

Goode, E. E., & Wagner, B. (1993, May 16). *Does Psychotherapy Work? The language of therapy saturates American culture, yet questions remain about the power and value of this vast healing enterprise.* . Retrieved May 30, 2011, from US News and World Report: http://www.usnews.com/usnews/culture/articles/930524/archive_015192_6.htm

H., Doug . (2011, June 4). Saturday Night Speaker Meeting, Apple Valley, CA.

Harvard Medical School. (10-2007, October). The Spiritual Side of Recovery. *Harvard Mental Health Letter, 24*(4), p. 6.

Harvard Medical School. (1-2009, January). Alcohol Abstinence vs. Moderation: Degree of dependence predicts which strategy works best. *Harvard Mental Health Letter*, p. 6.

Harvard Medical School. (3-2005, March). The Nocebo Response. *Harvard Mental Health Letter*, pp. 6-7.

Harvard Medical School. (5-2008, May). Behavioral Cognitive Therapy for Addictions. p. 5.

Harvard Medical School. (5-2011, May). *Understanding the "nocebo" effect, from the Harvard Mental Health Letter*. Retrieved June 3, 2011, from Harvard Health Publications: http://www.health.harvard.edu/press_releases/understanding-the-nocebo-effect

Harvard Medical School. (7-2005, July). Drug Treament for Alcoholism Today. *Harvard Mental Health Letter*, pp. 3-5.

Harvard Medical School. (7-2007, July). How Alcoholics Anonymous Works. pp. 4-6.

Harvard Medical School. (7-2011, July). How Addiction Hijacks the Brain. *Harvard Mental Health Letter*, pp. 1-3.

Heagney, M. (2011, April 1). Study: Prayer turns aside anger. *The Columbus Dispatch*.

I, C. (1988). *Three little Christmas Steps*. Los Angeles: B&B Sound Recording.

Jones, I. F. (2006). *Foundations for Biblical Christian Counseling; The Counsel of Heaven on Earth*. Nashville: B&H Publishing Group.

Jung, C. G. (1961, January 30). Personal Correspondence to Bill Wilson. Zurich.

Keating, T. (1994). *Intimacy with God*. New York: The Crossroads Publishing Company.

Krucoff, M. W., Crater, S. W., Gallup, D., Blankenship, J. C., Cuffe, M., Guarneri, M., et al. (2005, July 16). Music, imagery, touch, and prayer as adjuncts to interventional cardiac care: the Monitoring and Actualisation of Noetic Trainings (MANTRA) II randomised study. *The Lancet, 366*(9481), 211-217.

Krucoff, M. W., Crater, S. W., Green, C. L., Maas, A. C., Seskevich, J. E., Lane, J. D., et al. (2001, November). Integrative noetic therapies as adjuncts to percutaneous intervention during unstable coronary syndromes: Monitoring and Actualization of Noetic Training (MANTRA) feasibility pilot. *American Heart Journal, 142*(5), 760-769.

Merriam-Webster. (1999). Retrieved June 30, 2011, from Merriam-Webster.com: http://www.merriam-webster.com/dictionary

NAB. (1992). *New American Bible* (St. Joseph ed.). New York: Catholic Book Publishing Corporation.

NAB. (2002). *New American Bible* (St. Joseph ed.). New York: Catholic Book Publishing Corp.

New York Times. (2006, March 31). Long-Awaited Medical Study Questions the Power of Prayer. *New York Times*.

O'Mathuna, D. P. (1999, Summer). Prayer Research: What are We Measuring? *Journal of Christian Nursing, 16*(3), 17-21.

O'Neal, H. (2011). *Codependency among health care professionals: Is an understanding of codependency issues important to the therapeutic counseling process?* Retrieved June 30, 2011, from Breining Institute: http://breining.edu/JAD11bHSO.pdf

O'Neal, HS. (2011). *Genetic Predisposition: A Review of Primary Chemical Addictions, their Etiology and Possible Implications for Treatment and Recovery*. Retrieved August 8, 2011, from Breining Institute: http://breining.edu/JAD11HSO.pdf

Physorg.com. (2007, March 14). *Does God answer prayer? ASU research says 'yes'*. Retrieved August 7, 2011, from Physorg.com: http://www.physorg.com/news93105311.html

Quenqua, D. (2011, July 10). Rethinking Addiction's Roots, and Its Treatment. *New York Times*.

St. Augustine, o. H. (1979). De libero arbitrio: free choice. In W. A. Jurgens, *The faith of the early fathers* (Vol. 3, pp. 38-40). Collegeville: The Liturgical Press.

St. Justin, t. M. (1970). First Apology of Justin the Martyr. In W. A. Jurgens, *The Faith of the Early Fathers* (Vol. 1, pp. 50-57). Collegeville: The Liturgical Press.

Waldron-Perrine, B., Rapport, L. J., Hanks, R. A., Lumley, M., Meachen, S.-J., & Hubbarth, P. (2011, May). Religion and Spirituality in Rehabilitation Outcomes Among Individuals with Traumatic Brain Injury. *Rehabilitation Psychology, 56*(2), 107-116.

Weiss, R., Griffin, M., Najavits, L., Hufford, C., Kogan, J., Thompson, H., et al. (1996). Self-help activities in cocaine dependent patients entering treatment: Results from NIDA Collaborative Cocaine Treatment Study. *Drug Alcohol Dependence, 43(1-2)*, 79-86.

Williams, D. (1999). *Scientific Research of Prayer: Can the Power of Prayer be Proven?* Power Latent in Man.

With Sobriety,
All Else
Is Possible

General Index

135, 138-141, 143-149, 151, 152, 154, 156, 157, 159, 161-163, 165, 167, 168.

Religions (other than Christian): 6, 8, 29, 127.

Religious Approach: (See Counselor, Religious Approach).

Remedy: 1, 35, 59, 61, 62, 70, 71, 75, 76, 106, 107, 112, 117, 137, 139, 146.

Resentment: 63, 64, 105, 124.

Rowland H: 72, 73.

Secrets: 55, 105.

Secular-Scientific Approach: (See Counselor, Secular-Scientific Approach).

Silent Contemplation: 53, 57-59.

Sloan, Richard: 130.

Smith, Bob: 5.

Sobriety: 18, 51, 62, 67, 69, 70, 100, 103, 107, 111, 113, 117, 136, 144, 148, 149, 157, 159, 167, 169.

Solution: 3, 4, 8, 50, 62, 63, 65-67, 70, 73, 80-85, 87, 98, 104-106, 112, 114, 119, 141, 144, 146, 153, 162, 163, 169.

Spirit: 23, 26-31, 40, 43, 47, 52, 56, 64, 66, 73-76, 79, 80, 82, 87, 90, 94, 95, 120-122, 138, 149, 158, 159.

Spiritus and Spiritum: 43, 73.

Spiritual Approach: (See Counselor, Spiritual Approach).

Spirituality: 5, 6, 21, 23, 24, 31, 36, 39-42, 66, 74, 95-98, 104, 107, 123, 127, 128, 131, 134, 138, 140, 150, 153, 161.

Spiritual Experience: 13, 47, 49, 50, 57, 59, 62, 70, 72, 73, 97, 102, 114, 119, 144, 163.

Thacher, Ebby: 18.

Tidwell, Rev. Greg: 133.

Treatment: 1, 3, 12, 16, 19, 27, 62, 71, 79, 80, 81, 83, 84, 86, 87, 88, 91, 93, 96, 99, 127, 131, 137, 141, 144, 146, 147, 149, 150, 151, 155, 156, 164.

Truth: 13, 14, 21, 22-26, 92, 93, 96, 99.

Willingness: 47, 50-52, 65, 66, 75, 86, 87, 98, 107, 119, 163.

Wilson, Bill: 18, 73.

Wright, Tom: 130.

12 Step Programs: 2, 14, 39, 46, 52, 55, 56, 75, 81, 83, 88, 97-100, 104, 106, 107, 111, 118, 123-125, 135, 136, 141, 143, 147-150, 161, 163, 164.

www.ingramcontent.com/pod-product-compliance
Lightning Source LLC
Chambersburg PA
CBHW060851280326
41934CB00007B/1000